The Innovation of HRM

The Innovation of HRM

Qassim Jamal Hassan

PARTRIDGE

Copyright © 2017 by Qassim Jamal Hassan.

cover image: www.freedigitalphotos.net

ISBN:	Softcover	978-1-5437-4066-0
	eBook	978-1-5437-4065-3

All rights reserved. No part of this book may be used or reproduced by any means, graphic, electronic, or mechanical, including photocopying, recording, taping or by any information storage retrieval system without the written permission of the author except in the case of brief quotations embodied in critical articles and reviews.

Because of the dynamic nature of the Internet, any web addresses or links contained in this book may have changed since publication and may no longer be valid. The views expressed in this work are solely those of the author and do not necessarily reflect the views of the publisher, and the publisher hereby disclaims any responsibility for them.

Print information available on the last page.

To order additional copies of this book, contact
Toll Free +65 3165 7531 (Singapore)
Toll Free +60 3 3099 4412 (Malaysia)
orders.singapore@partridgepublishing.com

www.partridgepublishing.com/singapore

Contents

Abstract 6

Preface 8

UNIT One
THE History Of HRM 11

UNIT Two
THE Frame of HRM in the Organization 20

UNIT Three
THE International HRM Strategies, During foundation,
Drowning & Practices 41

UNIT Four
THE I-HRM in Selection & Managing The Financial Strategies for the
International organizations 55

UNIT Five
THE I-HRM in Selection & Managing The Organizations Cultures 80

UNIT Six
THE HRM in Selection & Managing The Organization Performance 105

References 133

Abstract

Normally, the organizations Managers could reflect some conflicts or crises actions, regarding their performance or interactions within their organization, goals and activities. Suppose their high qualifications and knowledge. Therefore, they should be more able to reform their organizations performance and goals by support, the managing of their organizations, regarding details and information. Rather than, managing any classical performance frame, to avoid any misunderstanding, between, the organization management and staff, or staff with management. Thus, The HRM field in an organization is involved, to reflect the organizations mechanisms during information. Updating. Also reform the staff performance in a smooth way. to support the organizations sustainably during the performance and attitude within markets. Therefore, this book is founded to support the organizations managers, regarding their actions and decision making, suppose if they are beginners or midlevel. In The same way, this book will support the HRM researchers to recommend the integration journey for the HRM, in the organizations in founding, updating, reforming and add the talents actions for the organizations. In the same way, this book will add more information For the HRM students and researchers. regarding the Concepts, actions, and practical strategies for the HRM Journey and interactions within the organizations. Especially the international organizations. Because the organizations Managers could reflect some conflicts or crises actions, regarding their performance or interactions within their organization, goals and activities. Suppose their high qualifications and knowledge. Therefore, they should be more able to reform their organizations performance and goals by support, the managing of their organizations, regarding details and information. Rather than, managing any classical performance frame, to avoid any misunderstanding, between, the organization management and staff, or staff with management. For this, The HRM field in the organization is involved, to reflect, the organizations updating and reforming in smooth way, to support the organizations sustainably during the performance and attitude within markets, Therefore, this book is founded to support the organizations managers, regarding their actions and decision making, suppose if they are beginners or midlevel. In The same way, this book will support the HRM researchers to recommend the integration journey for the HRM, in the organizations in founding, updating, reforming and add the talents actions for the organizations. In the same way, this book will add more information For the HRM students and researchers, regarding the Concepts, actions, and practical currents-strategies for the HRM Journey and interactions within the organizations, especially the international organizations because of it complex mechanisms in performance and targets.

Preface

During the Eve of 21 century, The organizations managers are trying seriously to integrated their organization targets & needs, to convey the organization message in clear way within the business Sectors, to alliance more profits and benefits regarding their organization activities and performance. For this issue, the goad using of HRM scope in the organization performance, will support, the integration current of It activity and performance for example, because of the complex implementation within the organizations in consuming productions and items. Thus, every organization management is trying to it best effort in managing the HRM during it integration norms because the real capital for the organization is it staff and worker. For this, the modern firms are Trying to lay the motivation and trust scoops within it performance environment to support the organization, In matching It targets and needs, and providing more opportunities for organization to support it outcomes. Therefore, the drawing of clear frame regarding the staff integration within some tools like: strategic, administrative, informational, development during continuously actions will applying the concept of performance management system, within The HRM activities during the organization performance. For this issue, the principles of HRM are required to focusing in serious way during some important issues regarding the journey of staff improvement in the organization performance, To guide the improvement advantages within organization improvement currents by support the organization Values and behaviors, during the staff interactions and performance. To do this in smooth way, the organization management should improve the staff ability to understand the organization mission and goals, because the clear understanding of the organization targets will guide the employee's performance to match the organization goals and support the organization out source, during the duties coordination between top management & staff. In the same way, the HRM principles are required to applying the performance management system within the organizations mechanism. By providing the scopes of clear information about, the staff duties and the organization rules, to support the acceptance norms, for the organizations mechanism and targets. After that, they are required, for introducing more superiors skills or talent in changing and reforming the Working activates and the mechanism for the organization performance, to avoid any performance leakage, or any managerial dilemma, by selecting some actions or techniques. Like: using the flexible discussion between management and the staff. In the same way, The organization management should using the performance appraisal to recommending any weakness or performance leakage in the organization system. In the same way, the mission of HRM in reforming and supporting the organizations performance and targets is not so easy because of some rezones. Like:

1- Conflicts between staff and their organization management.
2- Bad coordination for duties arrangement.
3- Miscommunication in the organization environment.
4- The weakness of measuring systems for the staff performance.
5- Updating the modern information and technologies materials.
6- Selecting and reform the organizations strategies.
7- Interring and interact with global markets.

For this, The HRM in any modern organization, are locking for the staff or employees, as important capital, wish need to reform and support, before reflect any innovation or integration action or performance during their organizations environments, by conveying the organization targets within tactfully currents, to match the minds and behaviors for the organizations staff. In the same way, the HRM, in any organization are able resolve any conflict between the organization and staff. Alternatively, the staff with the organization during some smart techniques, like: recommending the weakness chains during the interaction between the organization and staff. By making performance appraisal or any similar actions to set some clear points, regarding the relation between the employee and organization, Therefore, the HRM, are able to reflect the juice of their experiences and qualifications within organization environment to push the mechanism of the organization in interring the global markets within safe currents and adding more values for the international organization in matching the scope of hybrid needs and completions in this new environment. Finally, if we assume that, the HRM is like a tree we needs, to analysis this tree from its roots, till it leaves, to recommend, the shadow of the implantation and integration, for any successful organization

UNIT One
THE History Of HRM

Introduction
The History of HRM

Indeed the history of HRM foundation was starting in the USA during the "18" century, to support two importing targets: The first target is to support the integration scope of US manufactures in productions and distributing. The scorned target is to avoid any capitals leakage, to other nations. Like, Europe nations or any other nations. For this, the main equation of HRM is focusing about the capitals saving & reforming, even if the capitals are related to currency or human performance. On other hand, in the '1877, the mangers of US organizations are starting, to draw a clear frame about the labors needs & performance to match their different Mentalities and trends with, the organizations environments to support the US organizations targets and needs. In the same way, the organization managers in the USA are focusing seriously about the labors performance in manufactures an environment. Because of the growth for the labors numbers, in US, which reflect a deferent needs and performance skills to manage this huge scope of labors requirements? Whish guide them to accelerating the numbers of Mangers & Assistants, to guide and protected the labor performance within firms. For this issue, the drowning of clear frame, about the labors rights and rules to match their performance, with US organizations environment, is a very important action to support the US organizations regarding their innovation & integration. For this issue, the trend of HRM is starting to found a good place in the US organizations, to achieve the organization targets and needs. Also, support the trust scales of capitals confidence for all US, investors. Even if they are locals or foreign, To keep the US capitals running in the safe cycle, For this nice issue, the US is passing to reflect the philosophy, of HRM reforming, by making some talent actions.

For example, The' US government', was making an agreement with some low scholar. Like:' Henry Town & George Patterson' to establish the US labors low in the 'US' organizations & markets, to achieving some goals. Like: introducing rules about the labors and their relation and rights within US organizations, to saving the rights of the two parties And support The relationship between management and the industrial section, To broke all contracts off classic markets trends, by shaping a new scope, of organizations performance during the staff actions and interactions with their duties and activities. For this, the bottom of challenging was occurring during the transferring of the classical trend for the US organizations to the modern scope and how could the globalization support this new issue to match the new performance for the managers, staff & labors in the organizations? Especially In impressing the international organizations? For this issue, the sweeping of tradition contrast of American economic should running through practical mechanism to support the modern conceptual of HRM, by adding more values & trends within, the staff and labors performance And behaviors, during their interactions within their organizations environments. Thus, the practical actions were starting, by introducing The section of 'labor management relations on 1900.

The main goals of this section are to support the skills of mangers and leaders, skills and performance to reflect more integration & innovation for the staff and labors performance and behaving within the US organizations. to match all needs of the modern organizations scope in the supplying & demands within the US markets. For this, It will be an easy issue to recognizing that, the reforming of mangers & staff performance will support the mechanism of domestic & international markets. Because, the improving mangers scope in HRM scope, will create a strong current Of performance during the conceptual and the practical currents. By reflecting all of the experiences and skills to support the organizations to match all goals and targets during the current goals and future goals, by matching all changing and updating for the markets needs and requirements. Because, more knowledge and experiences will support the organizations to support it productions quality and to expect the future needs for this productions. In the same way, the safety and flexible Environments for the organization will impressing the labors performance in comfortable way to distribute their Performance within clear mechanism to support the organization needs and targets. Finally, the safety and comfortable working environment will support the roots of creating and developments for the managers, assistants and labors regarding their performance and actions in the organizations, On other hand we could said that, If the organizations staff and mangers, are knowing will about their: rights, duties and performance. And their loyalty for the organizations, Thus, Their attitude and performance will growth, regarding, their interactions within their organizations. In the same way, if the organization management is passing to sweep any conflict or dilemma in the organization Environment the scope of crating and innovation in the organization performance. For this issue the philosophy of HRM, In the USA, was starting in strong and clear way, to reflect more achievements for the US organizations by reforming the soul of humans within the organizations, actions and goals.

Example 1.1

In the 1900, the cigar factor management In the Boston city was trying to break the classic contrast, of managing labors performance. By doing some smart actions like: classifying the labors, in two levels. The first level is the skilled labors. And the second level is the non-skilled labors. To supports some important actions like:

1- Classifying the wags between skilled and non skilled labors in a smooth way, because It not fair to distributing, the wages between skilled and non skilled labor in one current.

2- Improving the ability of skilled labors to interact with complex duties rather than, non-skilled labors.

3- Dilute the conflicts and dilemmas, between labors, by making them working into small Groups, to avoided any problems or crises, during their interactions, of a significant number, for the factor staff.

For this, the growth of performance skills, in labors, of the cigar factor, in the Boston, is support, the scope, Of supplying and demand, for the cigar market, especially, the US markets needs, for the cigar, regarding, the quality and quantity, of this production in matching in the US smokers because, the comfortable Working environment is able, to reflect more innovation and integration, in the practical performance, in the organization.

In the same way, if the organizations are not able to support all modern needs, for the modern contemporary requirements and needs, to support its performance, especially: in passing, the labors problems. Like: the misunderstanding of their duties or the organization roles & regulations, the leakage of performance will be reflected in the clear way in the organization environment. Wish means: the destroying of the organization future in matching it productions and needs within the domestics and global markets.

The growth of HRM norms, in 1920

Actually, this important current for the HRM field is taking the benefits, from the previous interactions for HRM in the 18 century. Is starting, to draw a clear frame, regarding the modern performance in the organizations to match the basics needs for the modern contemporary requirements in imperatives and competencies actions, To support the anticipates for the markets growth. Especially in sweeping the estimations for the Classic management field. For example: in 1920, the introducing of the 'IRAA' field in the modern management wish meant (Industrial Relations Association of America). **(Kaufman, Bruce E.)** To support the US organizations in support its needs And activities during some smarts actions like: Establishing a counseling firms to support the investors in establishing A strong soul for their businesses activities. In the same way, the IRAA organization is introducing the first management magazine to update the US organizations mangers regarding the modern concepts and practical currents, in modern management field during the help of the 'University of Wisconsin'. Especially in supporting the large organizations performance in matching all of the domestics and international labors markets needs, because the philosophy of IRAA, is focusing about the labors as very important capital to support, the organizations activities and goals. On other hand, a qualified management is able to reform the performance of labors and the skills labors, to be more able to support the organizations goals and targets. In the same way, the philosophy of IRAA could match and support the large organizations activities. By reflect the scope of modern management, in managing the complex environment for the large Organizations, because the big number of labors is reflecting more positive actions and dilemmas in the large organizations

Example 1.2

In1920, The western Electric organization in the Chicago was establishing its new branch in The Australia, to produce and consuming, it electricity productions within Australia nation, But the management of WEO, was recommending, some managerial crises in this new branch, like The minimizing of sales revenues and the leakage of synergy between the staff and labors in the Australia branch. For this serious issue the management, of WEO in the US, was using the helping of one counseling organization, to selecting some modern actions to support it activates in the Australia. Like: introducing the housing allowance and life insurance allowance, for it staff and labors, in the Australia branch. For this, the integration current is return, to run in a good way in the WEO branch in the Australia. Because the new mechanism of the housing allowance and life insurance allowance is support the comfortable environment between the staff and their organization performance. In the same way, This mechanism is to establish a new current for the labors rights in the organizations, especially if the organization staff and labors are leaving their nation boundaries to work in the New host nation. Which mean, they are leaving their houses and families to the new environment?

(Kaufman, Bruce E)

Now it will be a clear issue to recommending that: the homogenization of the IRAA, in the context and actions is passing to reflect some important currents for the US organizations sustainability by enhancing the perceived for the modern US organizations tendency in the begging of 19 century. Especially in creating the best criteria's to support the modern challenges For the 19-century needs and requirements, especially in sweeping any obstacle in the organization performance and needs.

The Growth of HRM in 19 century

Actually, the reflecting of all the previous actions for the HRM in management fields, From last middle of "18" century till the beginnings of 19 century, Is to introducing and select the best actions and decisions Making in the modern organizations activities. Like: labors wages and contracts, to support the rising of this important managerial field. Especially to lay a strong soul for this important field, by create more integration and innovation actions within organization boundaries, to introduce more flexibility and rules to support the modern organization in applying it perceptions Regarding its performance and targets. To do it within the practical currents, by reforming any leakage current, of the organization performance and enhancing any positive idea or action. The main idea of this, Is To push the sustainability for the organizations profits and targets, especially in matching all performance currents and futures needs for the organizations. In the same way, the HRM field is introducing the best practical norms to match all of the small, medium and large organizations within the practical scope. By support the hierarchy systems for the different organizations and support the mangers, staff and labors needs and performance during the interactions within their organizations environments. By dilute the modern management concepts and techniques during coherence trends. For example: establishing the management counseling organizations, to reform the mangers performance and support the labors Loyalty for their organizations. To do it during some actions like wages rights, training and insurance for the organization staff. In the same way, The IRAA organization in the "US" is able to support the labors performance field. By establishing and support, it labors audit sector, in 1920" **(Kaufman, Bruce E)**, to support All labors needs and requirement from their organizations. By doing some actions like: Asking the managers, to explain the labors rules, for the staff and labors during the interview operation. In the same way, The IRAA organization, Is guide the performance for the laborers and staff, during, the best management techniques. By guide it counseling organization to remove any Conflict between the organization and staff and support the relation between the staff and mangers in the organization, by making an investigating for the managerial problems and introducing The best solutions to remove the managerial problems in the organizations, and making appraisal for the organizations in the US, to measure the relation-ship between the labors and their organizations and measuring the US organizations performance during it activities and achievements.

Example 1.3

In the middle of 1920, the HRM counseling organizations in the US, are introducing the labors welfare sector to support the labors performance and achievements in the US organizations, during it performance and competitions in productions and supplying. In the same way, the philosophy of this sector is looking for the organizations labors as important capital. Wish need is supporting and reform, to take some revenues during some long actions and plans. For this issue, the welfare sector, was selecting some smart actions to support the labors loyalty and performance for their organizations like: creating functional staff departments, old age pensions and job security. In the same way, the HRM counseling organizations was starting in this time, to introduce some hypotheses and empirical studies regarding the motion performance for Labors and staff in the US organizations, by the co-operation of the university of Pennsylvania. Which reflect more innovation for the US organizations, in matching the successful needs for its activities and targets?

(Bruce E. Kaufman)

Case analyzing:

Indeed, The above example is showing us the reflect of welfare sector, in guiding the labors and staff performance in smooth way with the US organizations, during long plans and actions to support The staff and labors loyalty for their organizations, Because the loyalty in the organization is the golden key for the organizations, to lay the acceptant norms between the organizations workers and the organizations environments. Because, the comfortable environment in the organizations will support the organizations to convey it performance purposes and targets, to match the mentalities of its workers. In the same way, a comfortable working environment will support the acceptant scales from the staff and labors To accept their duties, training in a good way. Because, they are believing will that, they are not working lonely, and they are will never be the losers if they are introducing the best effort and performance for their organizations. Because, the job security will introduce for them the best safety currents during their interactions with their organizations and the old age pensions will introduce a good revenues for the Organizations workers if their ages are not helping them to introducing more efforts or works for their organizations. For this issue, the welfare system is introducing the good basic actions in supporting the relationship and performance between the" US" organizations and it staff & labors.

UNIT Two

THE Frame of HRM in the Organization

Introduction

In unit one, we are recommending that, The Field of HRM was focusing seriously to select the best strategies and managerial actions to support and reform the organizations performance and targets. By locking for the labors and staff as important renewable capital for the organizations, which need more and more support and reforming to take the best benefits of this capital. In the same way, the HRM can introduce the best flexible currents, to match the modern contemporary needs and requirements. Especially in matching the implementation for the modern markets during it interactions and needs, to match the customer's trends for the organization productions or services with their different needs and mentalities to reform it profits and outcomes. For this issue, the philosophy of HRM was and still looking for the Humans in the organizations during their different mentalities, behaviors and religions, as good media in understanding the organizations performance and targets, To transfer those important conceptual within practical currents. Thus, the good understanding For the HRM concepts and practical currents, will support the organizations to convey its goals and performance massage for its staff, and labors, will reflect those massages to the organizations customers and consumers in clear way. In the same way, the organizations management should be aware during it strategies selection, to convey its massages for its workers and staff. Because any leakage or misunderstanding in strategies selections will reflect Crises for the organizations performance For this issue, the strategies selecting for HRM like: Planning and reforming strategies is not easy mission for the organizations management.

Example 2.1

In 1992, The Nissan branch in The Australia was reflecting a strong failure in adding any new values for its financial profits, during acceptance currents. Like: US and UK branches, for this The head office for the Nissan automobiles in Japan decide to close The Australian branch for Nissan cars In 1992. Which mean, the Nissan company will lose it Attitude and performance In Australia and losing more than 2000 persons are working as Engineers, labors and staff will lose the jobs? Thus, The internal investigations for Nissan company in Japan Are recommending some managerial crises wish guides the integration current for Nissan organization In Australia from 1970 to the failure scope. Like: the miss-cooperation between the head office of Nissan And the Australian branch regarding the performance protecting, for the staff and labors. In the same way, The Australian branch of Nissan is not supporting the modern strategies to matching the implementations Of others companies in Australian markets like, staff training and labors skills. Finally, the relation –ships Between the management and workers in the Australian branch, was running during the non-comfortable atmospheres, which reflecting more leakage during the Australian branch performance.

(Timothy J.Minchin)

For this serious issue, we could recommend that, There are several managerial conflicts, between the head office for Nissan in Japan and it branch in Australia, during the missing of co-operation and coordination to support the performance of the Nissan branch in Australia. Especially in matching the Staff and labors performance with the basic requirements for the Australian Branch for Nissan company. Which reflect weak performance operations? For this organizations performance in supplying, the Nissan cars, for the Australian customers, which mean: the leakage for the performance strategies between The Nissan branches. Because Of the missing in creating and applying The Nissan values and goals during within Australian branch finally, the Nissan organization could avoid the Australian crises if it select some strategies and actions. Like: Managing the Australian branch staff regarding their behaviors and interactions within the organization targets and needs. By explaining for them the organization targets, goals and how they could integrate during their working performance and support their positives behaviors, to support the organization ability to match its needs. In the same way, the Nissan organization could support the staff relations and interactions to avoided any conflict or misunderstanding in their working environment by introducing more confidence and trust norms and support the staff training and making evaluation to recommending any performance leakage, in the Australian branch to resolve any weakness, during the staff relation-ships and performance to introduce the best solutions and actions, to sweep any performance dilemmas or crises.

The Concept of HRM

The HRM is could be defined as, management field that focusing about the human's actions and interactions within the organizations performance. By adding and support the organizations, values, goals and rules. During the selections of the best rules, strategies and plans, to match The staff and workers, minds and behaviors to reflect more integration and innovation currents By understanding and applying, the organizations values and goals. In the same way, the Authors 'Holger Steinmetz*. Christian Schwens (2010)'. Are defining the human recourse management by saying that, "The Human recourse management is important practical current within the organizations performance and improving. Because this practical current is keen on the organization strategies and practices to support the organizations staff during their working participations". Finally, The Author, (Amanda Rose) Was defining the HRM by saying that, "The Human recourse management is a business field, which concentrating to push the levels of co-operation and coordination between the organization and it staff to maximizing the organization level and actions, during some strategic plans"

Example 2.2

The R&D is a famous international organization in producing and supplying the electricity items, within some Nations. Like UK and US. In the same way the management of this organization decide to reform it implementations within the international markets. By establishing another branch in Korea to reform the organization Values and profits. For this, The HRM section in the R&D is decided to introduce some strategies. To reform the engineers and staff performance in producing and consuming the organization productions within the international markets. For this issue, the HRM is applying some practical currents to reform this organization performance. Like: selecting the performance measurement system to measure the engineer's performance in producing the electricity items To support the production quality for the electricity items. In the same way, the HRM of this organization was selecting The empirical researches current regarding these organization productions. Especially in manufacturing and selling. To analyzing the modern markets needs. Especially, In what the customers could expect, from the R&D productions? Regarding the productions quality and quantities. For this, the R&D organization, was matching it targets and values by reforming It engineers performance and support the expecting needs, for it customs

(Bowon Kim*, Heungshik Oh)

The Case Analysis:

The HRM, In R&D organization, are reflecting the philosophy of crating the scope for the best performance achievements within Korea branch. By doing some strategies and actions, like: measuring the engineer's performance in the Korea branch, to avoid any quality leakage in the electricity productions, between R&D branches. To support the R&D productions brands within the international markets. In the same way, the HRM in the R&D organization is passing in good way to apply the strategy of empirical studies to expect the future needs from the Korean and International customers about the R&D productions quality and quantities, to support the value and volume for this superior organizations. Which reflect for it more attitude and profits during it performance and implementation currents?

The Selecting of HRM Strategies, In the Organizations

Because the main missions for the HRM strategies, are to reform the organizations performance and goals to improve the organizations ability to match all requirements for the modern markets, needs During the completion journey in matching and support the customer's needs from the organizations productions and services. For this issue, the essence of any strategy within superior organization is related on matching some important actions. Like: recommending the need of strategy in the organization. Especially in matching the strategy with organization environment, And checking the strategy Performance in matching and support the organization needs and performance. By making appraisal for the strategy plan in the organization in matching it purposes and targets. Because any missing link in the organization strategy will reflect some missing chains in enhancing the organization Performance and targets

Figure (2.1)

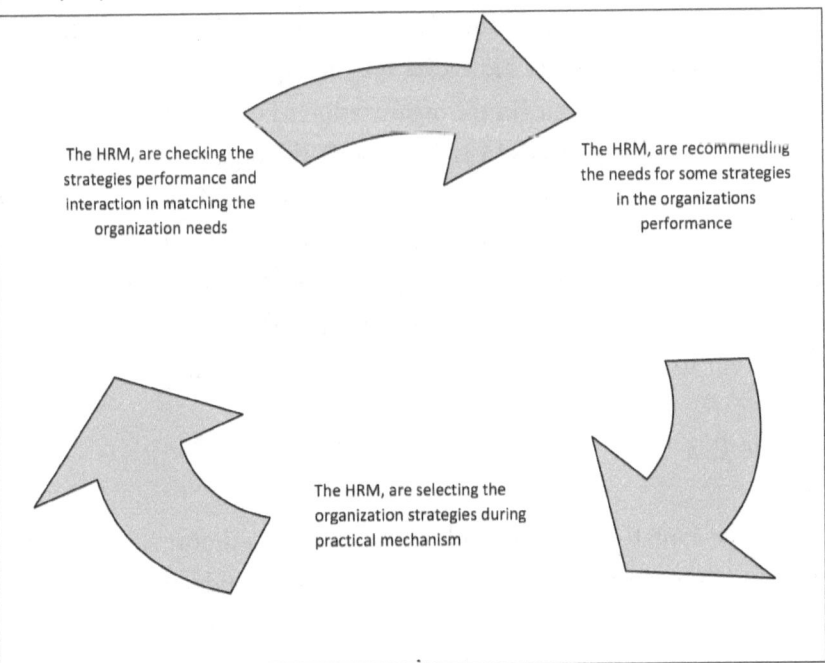

The HRM Mechanisms within organizations strategies

Indeed, every organization is having it sprits managerial issues. To recommending it needs for the businesses and performance for it new strategy or to reform its current strategy for several rezones Like: matching it customers needs, support it completions with other organizations or changing the organization environment. For example, if the domestic organization is entering the globalization markets or making other action, the performance of the organization is reflecting it needs for some specifics strategies to achieve and support it targets and goals. For this serious issue the HRM in the organization should know will regard: when, where and how to start the achievement mission. To apply any strategy within organization environment performance, For this, the HRM in the organization are required to select the proper rules and regulations for the organization strategies and selecting an flexible norms to support the best norms for the organization in matching the new rules within organizations environment. Like: management and staff to match the different staff and worker mentalities and behaviors with the soul of organization roles. Finally, the HRM in the organization are required to support and push the integration level for the organization value during the applying it modern strategies in the organizations. For this important issue, the bottom of challenging in HRM is Too match the organization strategy with its staff minds and behaviors. In the same way, the HRM in the organizations are required to applying some techniques, to lay a strong foundation for the strategy operations during the selecting and apply the roles and values for the organization strategy, to confirm the expecting goals and targets from the organization strategy in support the organization performance and activities.

Example 2.3

Initially, the Dutch police are working during classics norms till the year of 2000. Which mean: to catches The criminals and introducing them to court? But the government recommend the increasing of crimes and criminals. Because of the miscommunication and interactions between The Dutch police and the complex society., Because the Dutch society is running through bureaucratic life interactions with several religions and believes like: liberals & Catholics. For this, the addressing of social life interactions to support The Police mission in avoiding crimes and guiding the problems during positives solutions is not easy for the Dutch police system. In the same way, the Dutch parliament hazing unlimited power during some legal actions. like: investigation and reporting. For this, the Dutch government is planning to select an active system, to avoided any misunderstanding or misinformation between the three parties: the police, parliament and society, to support the Dutch government mission in reducing the crimes and providing and cooperation norms between police and society regarding sharing information and positive performance within the different members in Dutch society interactions. after 2000 the real changing of police system is starting to change by the performance of 'Pim Fortyny' by introducing more integration and innovation during the shaping of new government structuring of police interactions with crimes within several specific issues like: laying the performance measurement frame within parliament Performance interactions within political attention and actions. In a same way Pim is passing to distribute the shock of this changing by Supporting the performance management measurement duties and benefits during the peoples interacting to provide more opportunities for peoples to touch the different between classic performance and the establishing of the performance management measurement within Dutch police and other sectors during the performance values and interactions. For example, the recommending of performance reforming and changing in government performance during the public services and the old performance with missing of some services and information.

(, Lex; Marks, Peter)

Case Analysis:

In this important issue, the Dutch police are recommending some important benefits during the interacting within performance management measurement, by following the plan of 'Fortuyn' to guide the performance measurement during the practical norms within Dutch police performance. For example: In any crime like, social violence the suspects of those crimes should be introduced For investigation in the police station before they are presented to the prosecutor and support the political scope within Dutch governments. By making nice balance between the actions and the essence of actions during the police daily routine, to push the integration tool of Dutch police organization action for example: the numbers of fines are not reflection the police quality in issuing. Especially with big numbers, but the police Man should decide what to do and when to do this issue. For this I, could understand that, the performance management measurement is collection of important management operations like: protecting to recommending any weakness area within the performance chain, to provide the successful solutions to support the organization needs and targets for example, the performance management measurement is supporting the Dutch government sectors during smooth techniques like: flexing the fast integration and flexibility within government performance during the public services and provide the chances for the Dutch citizen suppose their different roots and information. To decide how is the government performance, before using the measurement and after using the measurement. In other example: The performance management within Dutch police sector, is providing the best arrangement between police and parliament like: introduce the criminals for police before prosecutor, to support the Dutch police in collecting data and records about the crimes and improving the Dutch police interactions with the complex society to support the Dutch police in avoiding crimes and improving the security of Dutch society.

The Strategies applying, for HRM In the organizations

In this sensitive current, the mission of the organization management is focusing about the creating the best managerial actions. To match the organizations goals, by adding more values for the organizations performance. In the same way, the organizations managements are requires, to insuring about the benefits of the modern strategy – strategies in matching two important currents: The first current is to insuring about, the matching of the organization strategy with the organization needs and targets. The second current is to cheek the ability of the new strategy in matching the practical currents for the organizations, especially in matching the new designing of the organization, with its soul of the performance. By selecting some talent actions to support the modern trends in the organization like: improving the technology scope in the organization, especially in supporting the technologies of information and communication. To support the organization targets in matching the customer's needs, by taking the benefits of Modern information & communication in supporting the organization performance. In the same way, the organization is required to support it productions consuming. By reform, it productions mobility for the customers and markets. Finally, the organizations management are starting to apply the concept of (out of the box), to add a new value for the organization performance. By appointing a new staff to work by using the internet or other social media for some purposes Like: avoiding the contrasts of working environment and taking the benefits of this new performance trend in adding the new ideas and talent actions for the organization, to support the organization performance in good way. In the same way, the organization management should be honest regarding its new strategy selection to reflect more integration for the new strategy performance by selecting the basics actions for this new strategy. For this issue, The Author **(John Robert).** Was introducing his argument regarding the strategy selection in the organization selecting in the organization by saying that: 'The Organization management should measure it performance in clear and honest way to reshaping the new strategy for the organization and select the organization trends for the production-productions, producing especially in matching the new strategy with it targets and goals. Finally, The organization management is required to show the expecting achievements for the new strategy for the organization staff to support the acceptant scales for the new strategy in the organization environment to reflect more successful norms for the modern strategy in the organization' **(John Robarts.).** In the same way, the organization strategy should focus seriously about the new staff performance in the organization by guiding their performance To match the organization procedures and activities. To match them within organizations needs and targets, by doing some actions like: introducing for them, their rights in the organizations. Like: salaries, vacations and promotions. In the same way, the organization management should introduce the duties and job descriptions for the new staff in clear and easy way. To draw the clear pictures about the organization environments for the new staff minds and behaviors, To support the organization performance and targets, by taking the benefits of its new staff actions and performance. However, the button of challenge in this issue is to avoid the performance mistakes or leakage, for the organization new staff. Because the experience for the new staff still in the beginning level, regarding the organization environment and performance. For this, The HRM of the organizations is introducing some solutions. Like: measuring the performance for the new staff in the organization and measuring their interactions and behavior, regarding the organization environment. Like: the cooperation between the new staff and their collage. To avoided any performance leakage or duties understanding. For this sensitive Issue, the HRM in the organization is selecting some actions like training programs for the new staff. To achieve some important targets like: improving the new staff performance in the organization and improving the ability of new staff in matching the organization strategy during short time, to improve the ability and capability for the new staff to reflect some norms of integration, regarding the organization performance and activities. In the same way, **(Herman Aguinis,).** Was introducing his argument regarding the strategies selection for new staff in the organization by saying that, "One of The main goals, for the organization strategy is to guide the new staff in the organization, To understand the organization values, to support the organization goals and targets". So it will be a clear issue to recommending that, The HRM is reflecting the Talent in the strategy Selection for the organization performance. By reforming the organization strategy Scales, To match and support, two important currents: the first current is to push the integration Tools for the organization performance and targets regarding, the normal staff. And the second current is, to support the organization performance and goals regarding the new staff performance and activates. Because guiding the new staff regarding their different cultures, behaviors and mentality is not easy mission for the HRM in the organization. Because the main targets for the HRM are to improving the new staff ability to understand the organization mechanisms while it values and rules. And reforming the new staff performance, to match the organization goals and targets within acceptable time, by doing some actions from the HRM side like: build a strong contraction of the confidence between the new staff and his-her organization. Because, the confidence between the staff and organization is like the Golding key for the performance integration doors in the organization. In the same way, the strong confidence between the new staff and organization is a result of several actions between the HRM and the new stuff like: The orientation between the new staff and the organization departments or sectors, meeting between the new staff and organization managements regarding expanding the organization performance and expecting duties from the new staff, for the organization. Because all of the previous actions are founded to support the new staff performance in the organization are founded to reform the staff confidence, regarding his – her organization, in it productions frame, it rules and values. Also, it behaviors to introduce some more scales for the new staff to work during comfortable environment to reflect more performance or talents in his- her soon future in organization. Thus, the main equation for all previous actions, are to sweep any conflict or miss understanding between the new staff and the organization. Because in sometimes the new staff is feeling worried regarding their new experiences in any new organization, especially in understanding the new experiences in the new organization regarding environment and performance. In the same way any misunderstanding or leakage between the new staff within organization regarding the organization culture and performance and the miss-confidence will occur between the new staff and the organization to reflect some arguments between the new staff and the organization management or reflect a bad performance from the new staff for His-Her organization, to reflect more crises or leakage in the organization performance. For this button of challenges for the HRM in the organization are introducing their talent to achieve the organization goal and targets. By reform the new staff loyalty for His –Her new organization performance by doing some smart actions like: make evaluation for the new staff performance to recommending the weakness areas during the new staff performance, making the organization culture more flexible to negotiate with new staff and the management should support, any issue be the new staff cases. By leasing for them regarding their idea and believes to motivate them, regarding the organization goals and targets and sweep any conflict any misunderstanding or confidence leakage between the new staff and the organization environment

Figure (2.2)

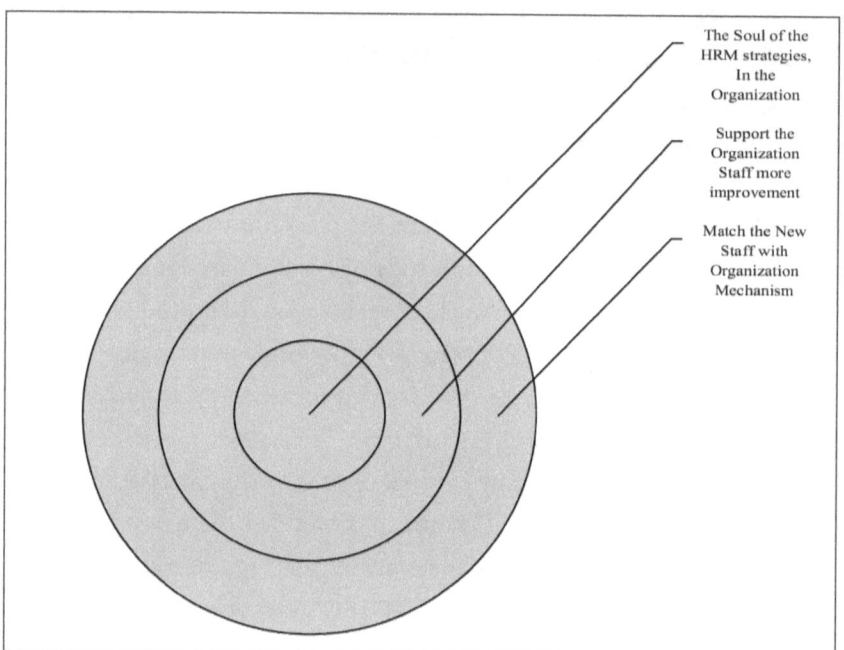

Example 2.4

In 1980, The Chinese organizations were starting to sweep the classical performance system in the organizations. Wish starting in 1949. To replace it by adding modern performance system to add the more implantation and integration value for the Chinese organizations. The essence of this new performance system is to focusing about the internal behaviors for the staff and workers in the Chinese Organizations like: Showing more respect for the organization staff, regarding age and qualifications with other skills for the staff within comfortable environment. In the same way, In 1990. The Indian Organizations are passing to alliance for more international businesses. Because, the Indian organizations are starting to make training for its staff during two levels. The first level is short Term training, and the scorned level is long term training. The purposes of those training are to matching two important performances current. The first current is to replace the traditional culture in the Indian organization, to modern organizations cultures. So the second current is to support the new staff In The Indian organizations with the organizations environment. Like: values and behaviors. Finally. In 2009, The Microsoft international organization was appointing a new 9,000,000 staff to working within its international branches in several nations. To match the requirements and needs from the international markets for the Microsoft productions. For this the HRM of Microsoft organizations are selecting some actions to match the new staff performance with Microsoft Organization like: making orientation, productions training and arrange meetings, for the new staff to support their knowledge and information about the Microsoft organization. To support The integration performance, of Microsoft in matching and updating, all international markets needs.

(Talya N. Bauer, Ph.D)

For this, the main approach for HRM in an organization is to matching the organization actions and conflicts, regarding it new staff issues and actions. To introduce the best performance mechanisms in solving any conflict between the new staff performance or attitude in the organization to support the organizations goals and targets. For this, the HRM in an organization is applying an practical scope to match the organization performance and organization strategies during practical performance currents. To add more values for the organizations Performance regarding the new staff actions and interactions, with their new organizations.

The HRM Frame in the Organization Culture

The Organization culture is critical aim in the organization environment and performance. Because, the organization culture is divided to the managerial actions, and procedures like: the hierarchy system in the organization and the staff behaviors mentalities and ethics within the organization. In the same way, the HRM in the organization is trying their effort to reforming and update the organization culture. Especially in matching the markets needs and requirements. Because the brushes of markets needs and the customers trends or expecting For the organizations products or services. Wish will guide the organizations to match the markets Implementations to update and reform its culture, to support it performance and goals. For this, the goad clarifying from the organization culture, and the HRM actions and interactions, with its internal boundaries. Wish will guide us to recommend the HRM actions and behaviors in the organizations cultures. To support the organization's mission in conveying their productions and services within markets, during the integration currents to add more achievements and benefits for the organizations, Regarding the organization culture, performance and rules.

Figure (2.3)

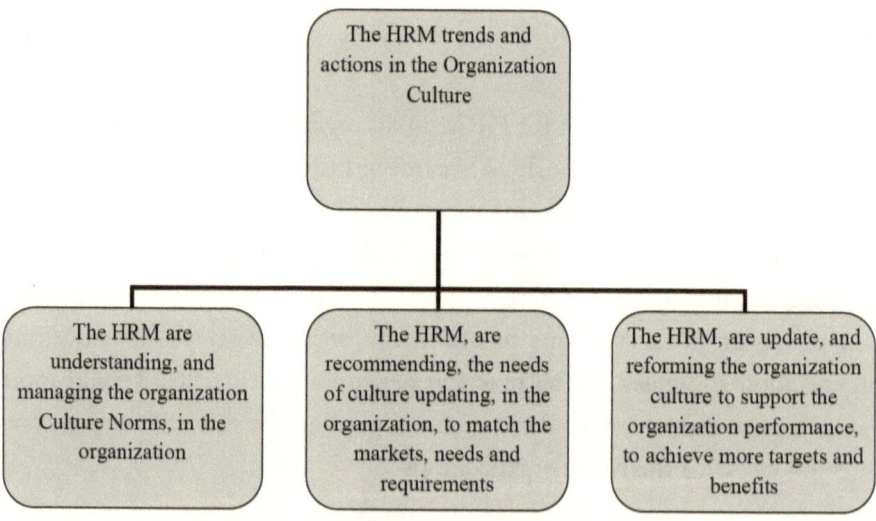

The Concept of Organization culture

Indeed, the organization culture could be defined as, the interactions between the staff believe, values and mentalities in the organization boundaries. For this, the performance leakage or the arguments occurring in the organization could relate, for some reasons. Like: The conflicts between the staff values or believes, by forcing keen on for some personals values or behaviors within organization environment. The other rezone could be related to a misunderstanding, between the organizations rules or actions and the organization staff or worker, values and behaviors. Wish reflected some bad actions or performance within the organization environment. In the same way, the Author *(Barry)*was introducing his argument regarding managing cultures in the organizations by saying that "The coherence values and behaviors between the staff in Asian organizations are passing to support the Asian Organizations to Alliance more foreign investments, to support the Asian organizations performance and targets". Finally, the Authors (**Pilbeam, S. & Corbridge,**), Are showing the integration current of managing, the organization culture. By saying that, The HRM managers in the firms are should be more able to reform the organizations cultures. By updating all of the hierarchy system, technologies materials, and adding the modern methods of performance to support the organizations in matching the modern contemporary requirements and needs from the organizations productions and performance". Therefore the HRM managers in the organizations should introduce an open and flexible norms regarding the cultural interactions between staff to the staff in the organizations and between the staff and the organization culture regarding, the organization procedures and actions.

Missing Chains between Organization staff

In unit one, I was explaining about the organizations staff as important capital for the organization because, the staff is very important source of power, performance and behaviors, in the organization journey during it performance and attitude in the markets competition. Therefore, the conflict or arguments between staff regarding some behaviors and ethics values in the organization are related for some reasons like: misunderstanding for the duties descriptions between the staff in the organization, and the hyper competitions between the staff in the organization regarding attitude and performance. Which reflect two negatives currents in the organizations? Like: the weak performance of the organization regarding it managerial arrangement. Like: staff training and duties coordination. The second current is the performance leakage for the organization regarding it conflict environment interactions.

For This issue, the HRM in an organization is applying two methods to resolve this dilemma:

- Method number one, The Classical method in this method, the HRM manager in the organization is using His-Her attitude and communication skills to force the staff to stop their arguments, conflicts, and cooperate to support the organization goals and targets.

- Method number two, the modern method. In this method, the HRM manager in the organization is more able for using more flexible scales to make the organization staff more able to touch the benefits of the soul of cooperation-coordination during their actions and interactions, within, the organization boundaries. By doing some managerial issues like support the coordination between the organizations departments, provide training for the organization staff regarding their duties and the hierarchy system in the organization. Finally, making balance between the political and official trends in the organization environment. Like: applying the organization rules and actions regarding the staff performance and staff behaviors to match the staff performance and behavior within organization environment, to sweep the conflict between the staff and add more values for the organization goals and targets.

Comparing between Methods:

In Method number one: The Reader could recommend some advantages and disadvantages for this method regarding the staff relations and actions in the organization environment. Because this trend of management is focusing about dissuading rather than persuading regarding the staff behavior and performance, Which reflect some missing links regarding the staff performance and behavior to resolve the conflicts of hyper competition and misunderstanding of duties in the organization. For this issue, the staff could stop their arguments or fighting, but during under the brusher current, wish reflects more performance leakage or at least losing the motivation for more achievement or talent for the organization performance. But in method number two: the reader could recommend that this method is focus about persuading rather than dissuading regarding the staff behavior and performance, To resolve their conflicts or arguments regarding, the hyper competition and misunderstanding of duties. Because the training, coordination and the flexibility in the applying the organization rules will support the motivation norms for the organization staff, to work and behave in clear and smooth current, by understanding the essence of the organization performance and touch the benefits of good cooperation and coordination. But without any bad brushed which improve the staff ability to reflect more motivation and talent regarding the organization performance.

Restructuring Strategies In the International organization

Actually, the modern international organizations are looking to avoid any performance failure or managerial crises, because of the bureaucry or misunderstanding or conflicts between the staff. Therefore, the restructuring strategies in modern organization are the golden key for the international organization promotion and development. Because the main aim for the restructuring strategies in the organization is to match the staff volumes with organization values and performance. To do this, The HRM are focusing about creating and updating the concepts and frame works of the hierarchy system and performance plans. To applying the duties rather than positions, wish mean, to support the organization performance by matching the right person, to the right place and minimizing the numbers of extra staff in the organization. Because, the minimizing off staff numbers in the international organization will introduce some important benefits like: reducing the international organization expenses like salaries and materials wish related for un-needed staff. In the same way, the minimizing of international organization staff will reduce some tendencies between staff, regarding missing cultures or performance during their activities and interactions with the hybrid society in the international organization. In the same way, the hierarchy system will reform the international organization decisions making or actions, by maximizing the decisions and actions scope during the arrangement of duties in the international organizations. Because the hierarchy system is like a tree, wish started from roots and ended with leaves. Therefore, the philosophy of Hierarchy system strategies in the international organization is to minimizing unneeded staff actions and performance and maximizing the proposals of innovations currents for the good communication and decisions making, for the society of international organization.

Figure (5.3)

Example 2.5

In 2008, The Board management for the American bank was submitting The new restructuring plan. To reduce the annual expenses for the bank and reform the bank performance in managing the constructions in the US. For this, The board management for American bank is deciding to terminate 30,000 staff. 6,000 from the high positions and 24,000 from the normal Staff, during four years, to achieve three important goals. The goal number one is Too minimize the mistakes off the bad forms regarding the contractions contracts between the investors and bank. Wish forcing some investors to issued lawsuits in the US courts. Against The American bank. Wish leads the international stocks market to minimize two cents, from every stock for the American bank. Because of the risk value from the miss-confidence between the investors and the bank. The Second goal is to introducing some associations currents with 'Crop financial organization' to support the American bank performance in managing the investments of constrictions. The Third goal is to minimizing five billion dollars from the annual budget from The American budget. Because the five billion dollars, are related for the terminated staff, salaries and expenses.

(Amirecan bank 2000)

The Rewards mechanism For HRM

Did the Payment reform the organization performance?

Initially, in traditional payment system the employee or worker will take his reward during His performance interactions within the organization hierarchy system, during three levels. The minimum level, the middle level and the top level, because of several reasons. Like: qualifications, experiences and duties within the organization performance. In the same way, the soul of this system is focusing about positions rather than performance. For this, the salary depends for positions rather than performance. So this payment system still applied in several nations like, (Korea & China) **(Aguinis, H)**. Thus, the traditional payment will make some conflicts during the staff performance within the organization. Like: making leakage in staff motivation, especially when the employee recommending the mismatch or the gap between his performance and his income statement, which decreased his ability for more performance improvement and integration, to reform his job in attitude and performance. In the same way, the, contingent pay plan is reflecting the opposite issue because in contingent pay the reward is related for performance rather than position. For this the increasing of performance will guide for more salary within the duties interactions for this the employee within the organization that' applied the Contingent payment, will try to introduce the best effort and attitude to reform his-her performance to improve his-her ability to match the organization needs targets. For this, the using of contingent payment system is related for some important positions and sectors. Like: marking sector or organizations managers. In a same way, the contingent payment is not solve or making any motivation issues for staff performance, because of several rezones. like: the misunderstanding between the staff information and the organization performance or the miscommunication between the staff and his-her collage during the performance coordination which reflecting some gaps during the performance chain in organization. For this, the organization management should be a wear about those sensitive issues especially when the organization management is recommending any gap between its mission and staff performance suppose the organization is paying more, because the high paying is not solving all performance dilemmas in organizations performance like missing of motivation or performance conflict during the staff interactions to their duties, finally The organization culture is very important issue in selecting the contingent payment plane for some specifics jobs by reshaping the staff behaviors and values within the organization activities To reform their performance during the organization targets and needs.

UNIT Three

THE International HRM Strategies, During foundation, Drowning & Practices

Introduction

In the beginning, The modern contemporary scales, during the implantation between the organizations are forcing some organizations to jump from its demotic currents to reach on the (MNC) levels. Wish mean multi National Companies. To wide its activities regarding of emerging economics requirements during the globalization frame work. To reflect more targets and benefits, for its new journey, For This, The International human resource management are required to push the integration tool for the MNC. By reform the ability and capability of the MNC to match the horizon of the international performance requirements For the MNC. By recommending the equipments for the MNC, and reform those requirements to cover the international scope for MNC during performance and behaviors in the international markets. For this issue, the good understanding for the I-HRM during the concept, frame work and the strategies, will guide us to understand the integration journey for the I-HRM in the organizations improvements, regarding the international scales. In the same way, the international organizations should be aware regarding others important currents. Like: the productions cost currency exchange rates and the customer's trends or needs from the international organization productions in the new environment. Wish mean: the host nation environment for an international organization management should avoid any managerial or financial crises. Like: the missed matching between the productions qualities and the consumers' needs or trends, and avoided the inflation or the gap between the currency exchange rates. For this, the international organization should analyses it new environment before establishing it new branch in the host nation, Therefore, the good understanding for the I-HRM during the concepts, frame works and the performance strategies will guide us, to appreciate the I-HRM Performance and attitude in the international organization.

The concept of (I-HRM)

The international HRM could be defined as, the controlling of the firm during it performance and attitude within it out-boundaries implantation by pushing the integration tool or the external environment for the organization. In the same way, The Authors, (Randall s.schuler*), are defining The I-HRM by saying that" The international Human resource management is the improving of the organization during its interacting with globalization performance and competition, by support the organization staff performance during some modern strategies to interact and deal with globalization challenges between the organizations.

The Selection of (I-HRM) In the Organizations (1)

The (I-HRM) is starting to interact within globalization trends for the organizations. After the middle of the last century especially in 1960, to match the growth of modern markets needs in the emerging nations. To take some benefits from the currency exchanging rates and reform the consuming currents for the organizations during the international trading. However, the globalization journey for the I-HRM is not easy mission, Because of the some managerial dilemmas in this field. Like: the poor facilities resources and experiences in this new field. Therefore, The I-HRM is starting to select some hypothesizes and empirical studies, by use and analyzing the data and records for some international organizations strategies and performance, to take some benefits from these new experiences. In the same way, the I-HRM is passing to support and reform some modern hypotheses in this field to support the practical performance currents for MNC needs and requirements during its interactions with globalization competitions

Figure (3.1)

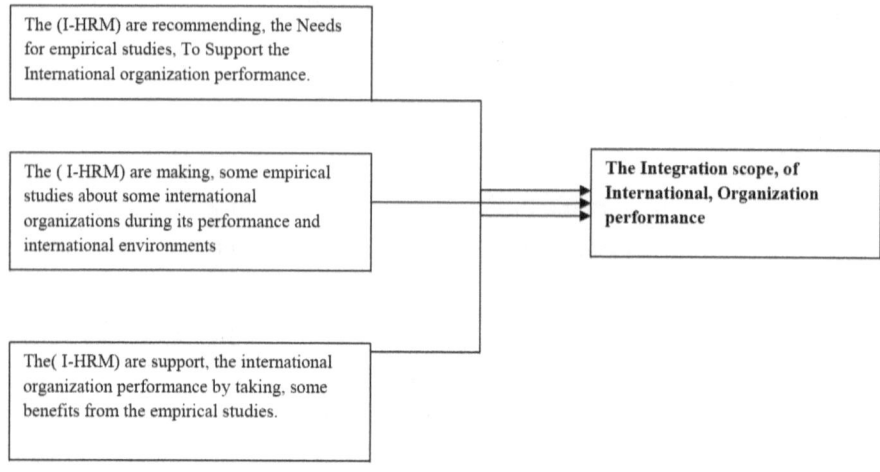

Example 3.1

In the 1960, The I-HRM researchers are looking for reforming the international organization, performance during it activities and culture, to support the new mission for the international organization in interacting with this new field. Especially, in avoiding any conflict or performance dilemmas during the new complex environment. For the international organizations during it performance influence. For this, the researchers for the international organizations from the I-HRM scholars in 1960, are the guide them to introduce a new I-HRM System wish named is (Nonlinear Dynamic System). To support the international organization evolutions regarding it difference pragmatics of hydride new international environment. For this international organization. Wish mean, the Nonlinear dynamic system, is founding and introduce, and support, the international organization, to guide the variable values and volumes for its international staff, with their difference behaviors and believes, during clear and flexible current, by restricting and reshape the new frame, for the international organization. Especially in selecting a new process and rules to support the new shape for the international organization. To sweep any performance dilemma. Like: The Trajectories of behaviors and ethics, between the staff within the international organization environment.

Especially between the Headquarters and the main branch for the international organization.

(Mark E.mendenhall)

The Selection of I-HRM, In the Organizations (2)

During the decades between 1970 till 1980, The Philosophy of I-HRM, was divided to match two important practical currents in the organization: The first current is to support and reform the environment for the demotic environment for the organization. Moreover, the second current is to push the integration tools for the organization. In matching the requirements for the globalization performance, to support the organizations in matching the hybrid atmospheres for the global competition currents for the international organizations, because, the computations between the organizations were growth during strong way in distributing the productions within international markets. Which force the I-HRM researchers and scholars to reflect more actions and performance to match the requirements of the implantations scoops between international organizations?, Therefore, the I-HRM was looking for reforming the soul of the organization environment, by introducing some plans and strategies to lay more safety for the organization staff during their performing in the organization and support the relations, between the organizations sector, to reform the organization foundations in matching, the competition of the globalization. In the same way, the I-HRM was looking to support, the organizations attitude within global implantation and Innovation by focusing seriously in selecting more global strategies and performance plans, to restructuring the modern shape for the international organization. Like: motivating, the organization staff and negation between the international organizations and support the virtual team performance, regarding the best using and updating for the technological issues. To reflect more integration and innovation, or the organization trends within globalization activities.

The Selection of I-HRM in the Organizations (3)

During the middle of nineteenths, the challenges for I-HRM was growth and running within huge and complex currents during the MNC performance, because of the reflecting for the modern globalization needs from the MNE in global markets. Like: arranging the operations of costing and pricing within global markets interactions. Regarding the assets and currency rates and push the integration tools for the negations between international organizations, to support the flexibility atmospheres for the international businesses agreements and expecting in advanced Levels, about the international costumers needs and trends from the MNE productions and items. For this, one of the important mechanisms for the I-HRM, is to lay an clear and flexible links between the HRM and the managerial actions within the international organization activities and practices, to set the numerous strategies plane in the international organization performance within clear and flexible scope to support the international organization, to matching the new variable for it journey within the globalization competitions and performance and avoid any tear for it mother and hybrid cultures during it interactions with numerous needs with the global markets. In the same way, the I-HRM in the organization should establish strong chains between some strategies for the international organization. Like: strategies of controlling development, structuring and the businesses strategies, to support the homogenization between the international organization sectors. Wish support its perceptions for the chronicles needs from the international organizations performance and implementation, to support it needs and targets. In the same way, the I-HRM is doing more talent actions and performance, by matching the internal strategies. Like: the strategies of organization structuring and performance with the international strategies like: international negation strategies, to reflect more invitation and integration for the international organization attitude in the global markets.

The strategies Scales in the International Organizations

Indeed, the I-HRM strategies for the international organization are showing more differences In actions and plans, rather than, the strategies, for the domestic organizations, because the universal organizations strategies should be more able to reform the practical currents for The international organization structuring, regarding the growth of the international organization, staff and managers and changing the shape of the organization performance during it, manufacturing and producing it items and services within complex and hybrid competition environment. In the same way, the international strategies should be more able to match and update all renewable and changing action within the variable environment performance for the international organizations, to support the international organization in achieving more goals and benefits during it sustainability journey within integration and Enovation currents. Therefore, The I-HRM should make filters to classifying the international organization staff regarding their different skills and behaviors to support the organization in drawing it Best frame work for it globalization journey, regarding it capitals and facilities to set the new processes and managerial actions for the international organization. Like: The information and procedures within the international organization. In the same way, the I-HRM should guides more managerial filters regarding the international organization culture, because the organization culture is very important tool to draw a flexible frame regarding the international organization staff during their behaviors, actions and mentalities. Wish support the I-HRM to read the common language for this hybrid environment, wish support the I-HRM in measuring the acceptance scales for the organization Strategies to avoid any conflict between the international organization staff, and any performance plans or actions. In the same way, the measuring of accepting norms between the staff and strategies could support the I-HRM in discovering the silent talents in the international organization.

Figure (3.2)

Example 3.2

The Philippine Batteries company" Philippines Company" is classified in the highest class for cars auto parts productions, because of nice facilities. This company that locates in" Barrio Bulac" in" Bulacan" city, Is producing Cars and batteries to exported to USA, CANADA, JAPAN, RUSSIA and THAILAND. In the same way, this firm is a partner with 'Ramcer' group For Investments. The main issue for this organization is to improve it integration scope., by looking to enter and to interact with the globalization currents, to reform and support it goals and targets. Suppose this nice organization is leading more than, 80%, for producing and consuming of batteries and cars auto parts in the Philippine demotic markets. However, the management of this superior organization believes will regarding the benefits and advantages, for the good performing and interactions during the international markets. There for, the HRM, in these superior organizations, recommend some needs for new productions options in global markets. Like:" plastic injectors' for the modern cars. In the same way, The total workers for this company managers supervisors and production staff are "517" employees. Almost of this staff is working in productions line, and the accounting department and the others numbers are related for managers and supervisors. The factor for this organization is around four hectares from

170 hectares that owned form Batteries Company. The most of managers and supervisors for this company are knowledgeable, because they have good Ideas about the Technical's Issues, but the important issue for this s Company it is still not fully computerized. However, this company get the ISO 900 certificate from Germany in 1999 and ISO 14000 standers. In the same way, the tariffs relaxation make nice Implantation environment for this company, the vision for this company is to face the Difficulties and challenges for our contemporary. Suppose this company passing others Asian company in production because it offer free maintenance and provide quality for it products But it needs some internal and external changes to make it more able to running during the hyper competition and integration current for it globalization performance. By selecting some important strategically questions like:

1. What are key characteristics of the changing environment?
2. What are the strategic imperatives that come from those characteristics?
3. What organizational challenges will be created by the new strategic Imperatives?

Actually, the Answering of questions is the first practical steps to laying the strong and flexible foundations, to reshaping the new changing environment wish started after the cold war in '1980', because of the universal economic and opening markets with strong implementation between others organizations. At the same time, The information technology have been growth and growth to be an important tool for the environment changing, because it accelerate the productions and distribution lines, In a same way it support the customer needs for what they won't and what they expecting from the new and moderns productions. For this, it is so clear that the essence for environment changing depends on the modern technology issues especially in information and communication that should be improved and update in the proper time.

Batteries Company was showing that, there are some missing issues in technology facilitates. Like: computerizing and production line techniques, which I will mention it later, When the improvement occur in a good way and the supporting of the nice e performance environment. Wish will guide us for more improvement for this nice organization. Like: smother innovation and the ability to find a new methods to form or re design the organization process but without any method that, could change the deliberate planning for the organization to keep the goals design ruining In the proper currents in durations and integrations.

For all above issues, there are some important strategic and Imperatives issues should be followed for the proper changing environment to control the Imperatives and the competencies to get the all expecting benefits for the environment changing. By selecting some important structuring strategies to support the activities and performance for the Philippine company within it new shape Like:

1- Increase Strategic Clock speed
2- Focus portfolios, with various Business Models
3- Abbreviated Strategic life Cycles
4- Create go to market flexibility
5- Enhance Competitive innovation
6- Manage intra-enterprise Cannibalism

Now, It is so clear to mention the importance for the increase the clock speed to improve the ability and capability for responding and follow up the new external changes and modern technologies issues. for example: Intranet system, wireless communication, to get more benefits and achievements from all this issues, by avoid any delay conditions to make the Duration ruining in good way, suppose the organization is showing an touchable changes in large business even if it enterprise or Complex. Wish operating to get all finance profit and benefits. But our new contemporary in modern firms showing for us, the new changing in strategic enterprise to guide all competencies in competitive currents, for smooth operating, by avoiding all the competitive issues. Suppose the management appreciate the different duration for industry progress, but the changing should be under the incremental and discontinuous authority to support any technical changing, because the repaid changes provide a nice and useful efforts for the industry circle for more better environment changing in this organization, by adding the flexibility for markets options, to reach markets Segments for more practical methods, the best practical issue for markets flexibility Is to select the internet options, because it provide a goad facilities with less effort and performance. In the same, t provide all information and options about the products Suppose the real concept for the innovation is still not much clear, but it is easy To find the innovation touches during the organization capabilities in classic or traditional innovation the innovation was focusing about two important tools in organization:The first tool is productions and the second tool is the process, but the modern innovation for modern company's and firms is focusing more about others important tools like: the firm design and the strategic improvement to accelerate the ability for improving the modern strategy and design to make all performance issues more active and smoothly Finally it will be an purposeful to push and support the production and distribution lines, by offering the best selling lens and improve the innovation speeds to grow the activity Circle to expecting about the new product duration in markets. Like:

1- Increase organizational clock speed
2- Design structural divergence
3- Promote organizational modularity
4- Structure Hyper Distribution Channels
5- Design material Research and development
6- Construct conflict Management pro cases
7- Organizational Coherence
8- Executive Team

Indeed, the fast responding from this organization management is showing the ability for organization capacity to improve the changing for markets, especially in laggard leading of the international markets. In the same way, the organization should focus more about others solutions for unprecedented speed to used all times issues in a good way. For this, there is some real challenging for the international organization integrations. For example, a good understanding for the quickening cycle to make a good advance for all expecting duties. In the same way, the goad rules and structures Understanding making all control issue done in nice way. But in some cases the firm needs to update some issues for the architectures to push the ability for the organization capacity., to passing competitive area in goad value wish need a highly support for real environment changing, by adding a different business Issues to passing more improvements ways. Nowadays the real implementation depends on abbreviated strategic tools to push integration Process for a nice organization design to passing this issue in goad way because it need to Depends and focusing about two important tools. The first tool guide all process and structures, throw long term circle during the organization value. The second Tool is to support the unique requirements for the organization. like environment and Culture for the organization. In the same way, the new implementing duration could take some more times to do it in good way. For example, before nine months, the organization management is required to Provide all structures to make it more able to provide more channels for distributions issues, to lead the markets. For this issue, The selecting for more modern Facilities likes: networks and multi options machines will make nice supporting for the organization because, It will help to solve errors in distribution lines and achieve some problems. The most important issues for the innovation requirement is to draw A new boundaries to add a new process and structures which expecting before. To provide high support for the developments issues. For this, the companies are a need to deal with multi-business will find some difficulty. For this issue, the best solution in this case is to add a good mechanism for the organization management conflict to avoid the environment conflict. In this case the good management is swept all conflict from the organization environment and used the positive conflict for markets Implementations. Nowadays no one will ignore that the modern firms operation Was growth and growth to untimed numbers for options operation and procedures which make the organization coherence a complex mission but it will be under control if it is under the culture and values norms and selecting a good enterprise. In the same way, it will be clear that the modern firms are running by several options and paradoxes which mean it is so difficult for one person. For Example, owner CEO to manage all this issues, for this the best solution is to activate the Executive teams to passing this dilemma in good way. because the Future organization which focusing about independent actions, will need the Executive teams to guide all important skills and actions to improve the ability To follow all innovation strategies in restructuring plans

Conclusion

All issues and conditions above is showing the new Internal and External boundaries For the future organization. Wish depends on the modern concept of imperatives and competencies keys in the international organization, to passing all innovations and environments changing currents. Wish feed all integration and Competitions issues requirement to lead the markets, but if we camper those Concepts and conditions with batteries Company. We will recommend that, it need more requirements To follow the future organization in many internal and External issues. Like: changing environments, increase the strategic clock speed, abbreviated life cycles,. etc. From the company history it need to adding more computers because it still not fully Computerized because this technology, will help this company for more achieves and Improvement after finishing the computerize issues and networking, Therefore, the company will start to adding innovation in modern way by improve it production and adding a new production to follow the markets needs like producing new line for trucks auto parts and improve the batteries productions, by produce batteries for Hovey duties. Like: buses and planes. For this, the company should focusing about the incremental and discontinuous changes for the technical issues by provide training for production staff to follow the new productions needs from the quantity till quality in same way To improve the number for cross functional teams. Like: supervisors and cross management teams to control the productions lines from A to Z. In the same way, the organization management for this firm could add modern facilities communications. Like: Wireless and modern faxes to improve the marketing department's levels, focusing seriously to sweep all bad issues or conditions that could touch the company coherence to guide the staff power for more performance and integration levels Adding all soft ware issue to control and monitoring the performance and back-up all data to use it in referencing and evaluations. To improve the innovation level The knowledge team should work hardly by arrange training for them and staff to avoid any negative for productions and improve the positives productions to improve the ability to expecting the customer's Needs to lead the markets, it will be more better To open new markets channels with others countries by provide some offers to take The new customers attention. Finally, the CEO will need more help and support from the new Executive team to guide all skills during the Innovation and integration Currents

(Training Knowledge Workers ©APO)

UNIT Four

THE I-HRM in Selection & Managing The Financial Strategies for the International organizations

Introduction

In our modern contemporary the organization managers are trying seriously to convey the integration concept within practical current during the organization performance and interactions, to reform and support the organization goals & profits. For this, a good understanding and applying of managing accounting & managing finance scope, will improve the organization management to reach on the best decision making regarding the organization Performance & achievements. Like alliance the customers for some new productions and improving the quality of services. For this, the Journey of managing accounting in modern global organization, was starting Science three decades. In the same way ,Robert is try to do his best effort and performance, to interact with Accounting scope, for several reasons like, analyzing the Accounting trend in organizations, by drawing the accounting picture in modern organization. Support the accounting norms in the organization, by adding the managing accounting values in the organization. Push the mechanism Of managing accounting in the organization by guiding his practical experiences in accounting within organizations. Finally, the matching the modern accounting scales with organizations futures, regarding the organizations needs and goals" **(Scapens, R.W.)**

For this important issue, (Robert) was starting in 1970, to reform the essence of managing accounting, by doing some actions like, making financial reports and statistics records, to introduce the measurements aids, for modern accounting norms. For example, analyzing the dilemma of inflation, regarding it reasons and actions, to introduce some smart techniques, in accounting scope, after that, in 1980 (Robert) was doing his best effort, to select the successful keys, of Manchester management school in accounting, by push the currents of hypotheses and empirical studies of modern accounting school within practical currents, to sweep the gap between managers and accounting norms. For example, making financial appraisals for 205 organizations in UK, to introduce, the modern accounting current in UK organizations, for this, In 1990, (Robert) was starting to guide, the modern studies in managing accounting like, PHD projects in accounting and management, to support, the integration norms, of managing accounting within managers performance and interactions with financial actions and issue, like, the effective of managing accounting with organization environment and the organization hierarchy system, to reform and support, the managers and staff performance, especially in matching the organizations with businesses challenges and requirements. Finally, in 2000 (Robert) was select, the professional interactions with managing accounting in modern organizations, by improving the accounting resources and actions in organizations and push The technologies scales within organization environment, to improve the modern organizations abilities, to match the future needs and challenges. For example, making surveys for staff performance and attitude, to recommend any weak performance, to select the best solutions and actions to reform the organization performance.

Management accounting

The management accounting could be defined as, the headway for laying any successful businesses, by analyzing all financial issues & information in the organization activities and performance, to support the business management, in the organization during any action or decision making inside it environment, to match the scope of business needs and targets. For example, changing the productions quantities or prices. In the same way, the management accounting, support the organization management, to reshape its distribution and consuming currents. In other hand, the empirical studies of Chinese markets, are recommending that, the using of management accounting currents, like,(S OES)system: which mean, state own enterprise is support the integration, of stock exchanging list and staff contracts, wish support the China economic.

For example, 'the first using of contracts with conditions was starting on 1986 in China organizations. By adding more values for the working performance like, bonuses. For this, the management of **(Iron rice –bowl)** organization in china, was selecting, the specific contracts, to support it management mechanism in manufacturing and productions.

Managing Finance

In this important current, the organization management, should focus about, its financial issues and actions in the organization performance, to support and reform the organization attitude and behaviors within markets. Like statistics or official financial reports, to meet the managing accounting needs, in the organization or business. For example, the international managers, of some multinational organization, are facing some problems, in adding the best value of pricing, between, the main branches and headquarters. For this, the financial managers of those organizations are deciding to do some financial actions, to pass this dilemma. By analyzing the financial data and records, in host markets for their businesses, and adding lists, For their headquarters, in local stores markets, for their investments, to support the value, of production unit, For the organization stocks and items. **(JOHN EDMUNDS)**

Differences between managing Accounting & managing finance

Indeed, the good understanding for the differences between the managing accounting and managing finance, will support the integration of financial scope for the organization regarding it actions and decisions making, because there are some different currents between managing accounting and managing finance, during the concepts and the practical mechanisms. For examples but not unlimited, the natural of report and official information is different between managing accounting and finance. On other hand, the financial report is running in general current. However, in accounting report it running in specific current to support the management decision-making in the clear way. Therefore, the financial reports are focusing about some actions like: appraisal or other similar issues. However, the accounting report is focusing about the management operations. Finally, the financial reports are more able to showing the current performance or business interactions. In the same way, the accounting reports can expect the future interactions or performance to support any Official actions in the organization. For this serious issue, The Managing accounting support the organization in it performance and mechanisms, to support it targets and needs. Wish improves the organization to handle and arrange its businesses and duties in clear and strong ways. In the same way, managing finance is support managing accounting, by adding more values and information. To support managing accounting, in matching the integration current for managing businesses and improving the customer loyalty for the production, by using the financial statistics and reports. For this, I could say that, the managing finance, is an important part of managing accounting to support any successful business. Finally, because the managing finance is the important issue to managing a business in the organization, the business managers should be able to interact with managing finance in the good way. However, if they are still not able for this, they could learn the basics of managing finance. Alternatively, using subcontractor's services to manage their organizations, especially the international organizations, during strong tools and actions, with save currents, to support the financial interactions, in their organization. Moreover, avoid any financial dilemma or crises. Therefore, the understanding and the interacting with modern accounting norms in the organization is not easy mission for the organization management. Especially in laying and introduce the frame of modern accounting scope in the organization. For this, the organization managers are required to translate the empirical studies and hypothesize of modern accounting to the practical current. To reshape the modern organization within accounting power and integration especially, in matching the future needs and challenges. In the same way the smarts managers, are should be more able to take the juice of managing accounting in their organization, by doing some actions. Like: reform the norms of decision making in the organization, by using the accounting information. Like: reports or other similar issues to support the future actions, of the organization. In the same way, managing accounting is support, the organization managers to Sweep any leakage in organization performance, by analyzing the accounting information, in the organization. Finally, the managing accounting support the organization managers to interacting with reports and information, which mean, improving their information and skills. For example, "In 1988, the japans banks are suffering from integration leakage and heterogeneity conflict in the interest rates for banks loans, especially in the variable of interest. For this issue the bank managers are using to analyzing the annual banks statements, at the end of financial years to recommend the financial interactions in the banks. For this, the banks managers are decided to do some managerial actions to pass this dilemma. The first action is to support the security options in loans to avoid any loan losing and support the percentage of assets in Japan Industrial markets, to interacting in a good way with inflation in local markets" **(Ronald E Shrieves).** For this, I could say that, the managing accounting is support the banks managers in Japan to passing the financial crises in loans rates and cash influence in industrial markets, by using the financial data and the communication between the bank managers to passing this financial crises. In the same way, the managing accounting is adding the integration values for the banks interaction with financial issues. By reform the security issues in banks, loans to avoid any financial leakage or missing chain in any financial transactions within Japan banks. For this, The Managing accounting is able to introduce the successful keys for organizations achievements in several sectors. Like: reform the organization performance in continually actions, by making appraisals or other similar issues. Matching the managers with the soul of management, by improving the manager's skills in communication and researching support the organization to match it needs and to face the challenges, especially the future challenges. Finally, the managing accounting support the organizations to reform it action and decisions making, regarding the financial reports and open discussion between staff and management.

Managing Accounting Currents

Initially in our modern contemporary of integration and innovations all organizations managers, are trying seriously to introduce, the best financial decision making, because, the best financial decision making, will support the organization to match the implementation current with other organization and support it internal performance & integration. For example, "The Hatfield organization for distributing the computers accessories was reform and support it net profits by changing it trend in purchasing from the supplier to the manufacture directly to take more benefits from, the productions unite price. By avoiding the fees of supplier to reform it net profits from this shortcut in Purchasing of the computer accessories" **(Lucas, M. & Rafferty, J)**Therefore, the good understanding and managing of cost and the cost currents. Like: sunk cost, variable coast and breakeven- point cost, will support the superior organization management for the best financial profits and decision making. Like: Cost, Sunk Cost and Brake even point.

The cost & Sunk Cost

Initially, the cost is important practical tool in the organization, because the cost is the headway for an organization to lay the selling price for its productions and services. Wish support the performance and profits for the organization. In the same way, the Sunk cost is the helper tool for the financial decision making within organization performance, by selecting the previous cost actions only. Which mean, the non-final action in decision making, because this trend of the coast is like, the binding contracts? Therefore I could say that, the sunk cost is support the organization in reforming the quality for it productions and support the exporting decision making for the organization to improve the organization ability in matching the markets size and needs. For example," the Swedish organizations of food production are using the sunk cost to reform the exporting profits for Nordic nations. Like: Denmark. by taking the benefits of common language, culture and the benefits of cheap mobility between Swedish & Denmark to support the costing profits for the exporting operations" **(Lucas, M. & Rafferty, J)**

Breakeven- point cost:

In this trend, the organization manager is required to making a good balance between the variable cost & fixed cost, to support the organization regarding it financial interactions & decision making. For example, choosing the volume of productions sales or bought new materials to support the productions units. For example "In 2001The US Airline company is locking to match the global markets needs and reform it profits, by using the break even points methods, by using the current of low-cost carrier. Like: low wages for labours, which reducing the firm expenses to 40%. Also, support, the firm to integrate its businesses, because of the growth of it cash flow "**(Peter Morrell)**. On other hand, the applying of full costing currents with its roots like, target pricing and price scheming, will be very useful issue for organization to reform it profits and decisions making, by support the pricing value for its specific production or services. For example "There are some organizations in UK, are using the (TVOs) method, to support the mission of breakeven points in the organization. Which mean, Target Volatility Options, to the alliance for investments in UK markets, because this method of pricing is able to draw the futures pricing for materials or items (GIUSEPPE DI GRAZIANO) In the same way, the organization management should be aware from any confusing between the direct cost and indirect cost, to avoid any financial crises or other similar issues in the organization environment. For this, the organization management, especially the superior organization, should make the capital data to achieving some specific financial targets. Like: support the financial record with markets needs, especially in updating the modern financial issues and actions and laying clear boundaries for some specific cost norms. For example, labours wages or material cost. Because the privatization of any specific production or service regarding the cost decision, will reform the organization profits and achievements rather than the applying of full costing for all productions services. Finally, the using of modern technologies. for example, the using of modern accounting programs, like (SCM). Which mean, Strategic cost management will support the organization to reach on the top of integration current? By reforming, the management decision regarding the production cost and the financial interaction. For this, the Author, (**Pong, C. & Mitchell, F).** Was introducing an argument regarding this issue, by saying that, "The marginal mechanism for selecting any accounting slanders within costing norms, should match two currents. The first current is to check the ability of this current in matching the future needs, regarding the firm performance. In the scorned current, the firm management should ensure the ability of this method in reforming the measurement tools for the firm performance to reflect some integration tools. Like: the measurement tool for any accounting method should cover the production cost. In the same way, this tool should distribute the overhead cost in clear and fair way".

The mechanisms of reforming the cost shortage

Initially, the reforming of cost shortage will support the origination management to reshape it price strategy, especially for interning the global markets. Because one of the important aims for reforming the costing shortage is to support the huge scoop for the malty differences for customer's needs and requirements. For this issue, the accountant scholars In UK are laying some useful issues to support the financial integration for UK Firms. For example" On 1988 the accountant scholars are adding some of the practical currents for (stock assessment), because the stock assessment is able to measure the full cost and overhead cost for production unit and pricing. In the same way, the stock assessment is able to push the performance of organization management, to push the level of organization benefits & profits. Especially in the using the stock assessment as measuring tool to measure a firm's profits, especially in matching the future needs, for organization"(**Pong, C. & Mitchell, F.)** In the same way, the using of (opening cost& closed cost) technique, will reform the stock measurement for the organization within clear way, because the Authors',(**Jianfeng Wu, Rungting Tu).** Are introducing their argument regarding this subject by saying that" The top of talent of managing the financial issue in managing the superior organization, especially the stock evaluation is related for organization management ability To manage the stock cost, regarding the best dealing and interaction between the specific profits In closed cost and the open norms of integrations. To do it in high-value profits in opening cost interactions, especially in support the managing of the stock volume and value within markets needs and requirements". In the same way, the Authors (**Jianfeng Wu, Rungting Tu.**) are introducing an argument regarding the performance of (opening cost& closed cost) techniques, by saying that" the empirical studies in UK organizations are showing that the volume of opening cost is running during the integration currents because of improvement in cost stock value from, 69.981 Dollars till 117,723,000 dollars, within fifteen years'.

Budgeting Strategies

The main target of budgeting is to push, the organization management regarding the managerial actions and financial decisions. By establishing a good budgeting plan and check the ability of this Plane, by measure it performance and interactions to support the organization needs and profits. For this, the budget could be defined as practical financial plane to support, the organization performance during it costing actions. Like: sales revenues and firm profits. For This, The managements of modern firms could support the budget control currents to reform it financial & managerial actions, by laying an clear current for it budget scope, by using the financial information to interacting with budget current and introducing the best flexibility to matching the budget concept Within organization interaction with practical current. In the same way, there are some conflicts between the budgets techniques and the practical currents in organization performance. Like: the mismatching between, the management decisions and budget, egarding the applying of budgets standers. For this (**Atrill**) was saying that" The weakness of protecting and motoring from mangers, regarding the budgets standers. will occur some missing links in applying, the budgets norms". For this, the firm management should introduce it budget plane during long goals and cheek the ability of those goals to achieve the organization profits during some shorts and specific actions. Like: using modern programs to analyzing the budget performance regarding the firm interaction with financial and managerial actions. For example, The using of the variance analysis method, will support the organization management to evaluate it martial cost and sales revenues In clear way, to support organization decision, regarding it profits and actions. In other example, if we assume that, the (X) organization is making contract with(Y)organization to producing the vehicles auto parts for five years. But after two years the management of X organization is facing problem with machines replacement, because Of inflation in machines cost. for this, the X organization will rent some modern machines to cover it production line, to support it contract with (Y) organization. But if the (X) firm is analyzing the cost markets for machines pricing, it could avoid this financial leakage by expecting the future inflation for the machines and auto parts. In the same way the Authors **(Christian Bellak, Markus Albrecht).** Are introducing their argument regarding the integrated of labors cost, to support the budget by saying that" the FDI organization is focusing to support the measuring of labors cost to push the organizations performance and improvement, especially in matching the host markets performance to interacting with large investments, by evaluating the labors cost with numbers of duties and working hours.

Accounting strategies In the global Organizations

Indeed, the organization could used the strategic accounting method to reform two important objectives for the international organization attitude in markets. The first objective is to support the organization needs regarding its targets and the second objective is to support the customers loyalty for the organization productions or services, to support the profit current within sustainability norms during the organization performance, especially to support the organization to lay it investment in host markets, to match the completions of productions regarding the prices and quality. For example, the analyzing of markets could guide the organization to reduce the production cost to match the purchasing power in market, by using some tools like, statistic analysis and financial reports to measure the market's ability and performance, to match organization needs and goals. In the same way, the organization management could support the integration of strategic accounting, by applying the concept of' balanced score', to support, the relationship between the financial and non financial actions within organization performance. For this, the organization management should transferring the measuring business and performance within practical currents, especially in supporting the strategic accounting scales. Wish pushes the organization performance and needs'. By laying strong chains between the organization tools. Like: financial issues, customers needs and the organization improvement. For this, the main target of balance scored, is to applying the homogenization between the financial and nonfinancial targets of organization. By using some tools like, modern technologies or performance reorders to cover more norms in organization performance. In the same way, The Author (**Hung-Yi Wu**)was introducing his argument regarding the benefits of balancing score, for the organization, by saying that "The balanced score is passing to lay the strategic map for banking sectors to evaluate the banks during performance and financial actions". In the same way, The Author,(***Daniel Revuelta).*** Was introducing other argument, by saying that" The R&D organization is passing, to integrated it budget and performance, by using balance scored, to match the financial current with managerial current within it working environment, by doing some actions like:

1- focusing about, the customer's needs and requirements from R&D organizations

2- Analyzing, the customer's needs, to support the innovation current, of the organization

3- Guiding, the innovation results and actions, within some practical points, to integrate the organization performance

4- Laying a flexible current, to match the actions of innovation steps, with staff duties and behaviors

5- Matching, the financial scope with organization facilities. Like: capitals and materials".

For this, the R&D organization is passing, to use the benefits of balanced scored method, by Draw a clear frame to guide the financial actions with nonfinancial actions during it performance To support it integration profits and it managerial actions.

The Practical currents for managing Accounting strategies (NPV)

Initially, the Net Present value trend in managing accounting is passing in clear way, to integrated the financial norms for the organization, especially in managing and evaluate the financial actions within organization, by doing some practical actions. Like: measuring the previous cash flows and generating the history of cash flow in matching the future financial currents of organization, especially during it interactions with cash flow in any investment or agreement. In the same way, the (NPV), could lay clear practical methods to support, the organization decision making during it performance, by measuring the capitals values and the financial actions in the organization. For this, The NPV is focusing about the pushing the scope for the cash flow and interest rates with continually practical currents and actions. Like: introducing the financial methods and making appraisal for this methods during clear framework, to support the organization management to accelerate the cash ability in purchasing or other similar actions to guide the organization in matching it financial targets and needs and avoid any future financial crises, by sweeping any future risk like, inflation. For this,**(Atrill & McLaney)** was introducing his argument regarding The NPV integration for the organization, by saying that" The NPV is working as measurement tool in the organization, regarding it financial issues and interactions to analyzing the long terms targets for organization during it financial actions, by introducing some strategies To achieve the organization targets and needs. For Example, A study by; **(T. Klammer et al.)**. Was arguing that' NPV is able to introducing a modern techniques for new operations in 80%decision to recharging the 60% in supporting the organizations decisions making, especially in the cash flow timing and the business targets. In other example "The top management of Friesland Campina Company, was making an agreement with Danube Foods Group to distributing the food materials during 41 years. For this issue, the management of Friesland Campina Company, was submit a financial plan to reform it benefits and avoid any financial crises, especially in matching future needs. Like: inflation, by making a discount for it cash revenues to match it integration and avoiding any financial leakage for it capitals and assets. (Royal FrieslandCampina,)

The Strategies of Transferring price in the International Organization

Indeed, transferring price is crucial practical current in the organization. Because, the organization is need to match it productions or services pricing with international markets needs and requirements, For this, the organization management should focusing seriously about the four important currents during the transferring price operations. like: variable costing, full costing, negotiated price and markets pricing, to improve the organization ability for alliance it productions or services within host markets performance and competitions. For this issue, the goad understanding and managing of the variable costing, full costing, negotiated price and markets pricing will reform the organization ability to support and reform it business profits.

Variable costing:

The variable cost is very practical tool in transferring price, especially in short terms actions for the organization that is appropriately applied when the selling division is not working at full capacity, and higher product prices. Wish cannot be achieved selling directly into the market. This can be seen as a short-term approach as when productivity is back to full capacity the selling division would argue for increased transfer prices.

Full costing price:

This method of transferring price is the focus about the nonfinancial actions to maximize organization profits, by doing some important actions. Like: measuring the investment level with organization divisions to support the organization decision making, For this, the organization management could take all benefits from full costing price method, by reform it integration operations within it activities of cut costs and drive divisional efficiencies. Since it is readily accepted that a business.

Negotiated Pricing:

This method of pricing is depending to the organization manger ability to persuade the second party about the production or services price. In the same way, the negotiation pricing could support the organization management to reforming it production value and quality to reform the integration scope of organization in negotiation skills and costing profits.

Markets pricing:

In this method of selling, The organization management is required to matching perceived pricing in markets atmospheres, by applying the variable costing for the productions or services and support the performance of its divisions to match the markets needs and requirements during the pricing norms. For this, the organization management should to be carried out effectively where properly identified taxes should be declared and accounted for the Profit sharing methods, because this important method, could possibly lead to additional tax as they could inadvertently the cause of prices to increase it to the high point, by the buying division may lose incentive to purchase from the selling division. In addition, backward flow of profits could also lead to loss in profit from transactions costs.

The Strategies of Inventory management

Indeed, the inventory management is crucial to the success of a firm and recognizing when to buy and how to store different items in the inventory is challenging? Also, when firms have inventory items showing different characteristics, like the slow moving, non moving and thefast moving items? Thus, the organization management needs to make conscious effort to regularize the time of purchases and the method of handling such stocks. For this, the good managing inventories, will support the organization to reform its current and future operations and improve the organization ability in matching it profits and needs, For this the inventory management is the value of service or item in the organization to match the organization needs& targets during it daily & future performance and actions. Like: the availability of stocks & transforming prices. In the same way, the managing inventories in the organization could run within three currents. Like:

Transaction inventory

This method of inventories is focusing to measure the client's needs and requirements by applying some techniques. Like: finished items or raw materials.

Speculative inventory

This method of inventories is focusing to support the organization profits during it financial actions, by measure some financial currents. Like: accelerating the materials values or finishing items.

Precautionary inventory

This method of inventories, is focusing about the consistently of the organization performance and profits, by introducing the basic materials and items for the organization. Like: staff wages & machines auto parts.

For this, the organization management is required to measure it inventories quantities and values, with it needs and performance, to support it financial interactions and strategies, by adding more profits, by matching the client's needs with it inventories integration and avoid any financial shortage or leakage, For this, the smart strategies In measuring and managing the organization inventories. Like: reforming the inventories levels during the cost and production processes. For this, The Author (**James**), was introducing an argument regarding the mechanism of inventory management, By saying that" The (MRP) strategy, which mean materials required planning is very smart method to reform the international organization during it inventories performance, by adding smarts values for the organization in managing it productions and items. Like: protecting the production values in the markets and introducing the supplying plan for the organization, by measuring, the markets demands with the organization productions and fixing the interval orders".

Example 3.3

Nokia Jumping to the Globalization

Initially, The Nokia organization was founding, in1865, in Nokia village from Finland during this time Nokia was producing the papers. In 1985, Nokia was changing it manufacturing trend, by interring the telecommunication markets, by establishing four sectors to support its productions performance. Like: mobiles and telephone sector, telecommunication sector, consumers electronic sector and information system sector. For this, it deserves an net profit of 215 million dollar. Suppose it used the performance of 44,000 staff and labors to match the domestic and internationals markets needs to support it supplying chain for it productions, during 33 countries. In 1993, Nokia was planning to reach, for the profits of 18 billion dollar. By reform it production currents to producing, IBM printers and other international brands

Budgeting process in Nokia Organization

Indeed, the Author was mention, the integration currents, of budgeting by saying that,' the budget is very important method, to reform the organization performance during financial working and interaction, because the budgeting, is able to reflect, some important actions within organization, like select strategic planning in organization, measuring the organization performance and integrated, the organization goals and targets'. For this, the superior organization managers are required, to select the budgeting current, by doing some actions like, making an clear frame, for the budget planning in organization, using the budget, as measuring tool, to measure, the organization performance, analyzing the measurement results regarding the organization performance, and applying the costing concept. In the same way, the organization management could take, the juice Of budgeting benefits, within organization performance, by introduce and applying some more actions like' laying clear goals and mission for organization, analyzing posts to matching the budget plan, introducing proper strategic plan, support the budgeting scope by collecting the proper information about the budgeting capitals of organization. For this, The Nokia management is passing, in a good way, to introducing, the integration currents, for it budgeting norms, to reform it financial and managerial performance, By applying some smart actions like, introducing it targets, matching it performance with it targets, introducing budgeting plan, measuring it budget planning by using the modern technologies and programs, applying the cost scope. Finally it reform it performance to matching, the budget planning within it long terms action and performance during some important practical currents:

Current number 1, the founding and interacting with budgeting & pricing scope

The history of budgeting in Nokia organization, was founding in 1989, when the Nokia management is decide to reform it sales and performance, by pushing it production sales from, the domestic markets to the international markets. Especially, the Europe markets, because of the natural geography, mobility and sales volume in Europe markets. For this, The Nokia was introducing it budgeting strategies to matching the international markets needs and requirements to reform it sales revenues and profits. In the same way, The CEO of Nokia is focusing seriously in using modern technologies and data capitals to reform the budgeting strategies in interring the international markets to reform and support all of hardware and software customizing to match, the international markets needs from Nokia productions. For this he was introducing his argument by saying that" we need to support our data capitals and modern technologies to match the global markets needs by reforming our local productions technologies and facilities to alliance our productions into host markets investments". For this, the technology team in Nokia is starting to create more information and talent during this field, by the management of Nokia organization. Wish was establishing a new sector to manage data, on 1989. Whish named data management section, to reform it productions pricing and quality and match the implementation of other international organizations in the Europe markets. For this, The Nokia data management was introducing an two important scopes to support it data capital integration. The first scope is named, data management producing and the second scope is named, markets ability for Nokia productions. For this, the Nokia organization was starting to reform it productions like, computers, personal telephones and computers, to match the international customers needs and requirements to support the range of it profits during it interactions within international markets. For this, The Nokia organization was support it sharing with Europe markets to reach on 20%. In the same way, it reform it sales profits interactions with International markets, by adding 1.2 billion dollar for it sales budget. For this, In this trend The Nokia management was starting to reform it productions profits, especially in computing sector, by focusing about the value and volume of computer chips, regarding it long term performance and it electricity consumption. For this, The Nokia management was laying a long term plan from 1980 to reform the computer chip, regarding the consumption of power and consistently performance Thus, The Nokia management is passing to reduce the chip costing for it computers section from 400,000 dollar in 1980, till 50,000 dollar in 1990. For example, In 1980, the management of Nokia Organization was spending the capital of 400, 0 00 dollar to produce one million computer chips, In the same way, it was paying in 1990 the amount of 50, 000 dollars for the same quantity, but in different size and quality, by adding a new value in computer chip production, which named (micro- computer chip) during it integration planning to reform it costing norms. In 1992 Nokia was, renamed it organization to Nokia mobile phone, by adding more values for mobiles industrial current like, introducing the first mobile in 1992 which working by GSM card and sending the first message in 1995 by Nokia mobile and adding the first computerized mobile in For this, the 1998. But all of those successful actions, are not enough for the Nokia organization, regarding it integration and achievement, because Nokia management was deciding in "2000" to support the integration current for it financial interactions and profits especially in matching the future needs and requirements. Like: inflation, financial crises and other organizations completions, by introducing, GPFA program to support the financial current performance and laying a clear scope for The Nokia future, regarding it financial scope.

Current 2 Managing accounting system in Nokia

Initially, the managing accounting system, is crucial practical tool in any organization or venture performance, because this tool is able to reform the organization during it managerial and financial performance, by doing some actions. Like: using the financial and managerial records of organization data. To support the analyzing results for the organization to the practical currents in the organization, to recommending the weakness chains in organization performance and financial interactions to guide the weakness chains within reforming currents in the organization, by introducing the best reforming plans. In the same way, the organization or venture manager of organizations could support the managing accounting system norms, by adding more values or actions within organization. like: matching the managing accounting system with specific plane in organization environment and measuring the organization Performance for it financial and managerial duties and actions. In the same way, the managing of accounting system, will improve the ability of information and data resources in the organization to match the plane needs, by choosing the best resources and facilities for the organization. For this issue, The managing accounting system, will match the organization benefits and targets, especially the targets of costing and organization benefits.. thus, the management of Nokia organization is passing in smooth way, to take the benefits of it costing and financial profits, during it Interaction with managing accounting information system norms, by introducing it best effort, in laying an clear scope for managing accounting system to support it efforts and benefits During it current performance and matching all the expecting for it future needs & requirements, by introducing a new managing accounting system plan from 1990 till 2000. Which named GPFA? Which mean, The Growth Profit and Finance Analysis For several reasons and targets? Like: updating the Nokia strategies in matching, the improvement of current financial producers and operations like, the growth of sales revenues operations and managing assets. Analyzing the taxes interest operations to support the Nokia in matching it future needs

The integration current of, GPFA in Nokia Organization

Actually, The history of GPFA was starting in the Nokia organization, by introducing the all researches and hypotheses, of "GPFA" To improve The GPFA opportunities to Match the Nokia organization strategies in reforming the targets and needs in managing accounting system. Like: generating future revenues. After that, The Nokia organization was starting to introduce it practical currents, by introducing the position of Global leader in managing communication of Nokia to reform the Nokia productions, by doing some actions. Like: changing The mobiles weights and sizes and adding the GSM card for mobiles networks to match the international customers needs and requirements. For this, the financial records, of GPFA system, in Nokia organization from 1991 till 1996, are showing the growth of expenditures rates from 41% till 54%.

Current 3, Managing Assets in Nokia.

Indeed, managing assets in the organization, is critical and sensitive issue within the organization performance, because the assets. Is the soul of organization capitals? For this issue, the main targets of managing assets in the organization, is to introducing an clear plan about the organization activities and performance, to improve the management organization abilities to interacting in smooth way with assets rates and returns, to maximize the organization profits and avoiding any future dilemma. Like: inflation or performance leakage in the organization assets. For this, The organizations or ventures are required to measure the assets planning during short and long actions, to support and reform the assets strategies planning, in the organization. In the same may, the organization should keen on about the investment duration for the financial transactions issues and taxes. To support it, cash returns from managing assets. For this, The Nokia management, is doing some smart actions to control it assets during short and long actions to generate it incomes revenues and reform it capitals, by changing it classics methods and programs in managing assets to supports it investments targets and needs. Like: maximizing profits during shorts and longs terms by selecting the GPFA program, because this program can introduce some modern methods in managing & measuring The Nokia assets.

Program number one, minimizing the rates of returns

The main aim of this program is to associating the investments expenses in Nokia with it revenue flow. Which mean that, the Nokia organization could take more benefits in maximizing it profits to match it future needs, by guide it purchasing department to bought more assets rather than any new items to support the Nokia assets to matching the futures dilemmas. Like: inflation, by discounting it contribution revenues.

Program number two, proportional depreciation

The main scope of this superior program is to applying the modern accounting practice in managing asset for Nokia organization, by supporting, two important financial currents in The Nokia organization. The first current is the expired expenses and the second current is the unexpired expenses to add All the benefits and revenues for the two currents in Nokia assets to reform Nokia abilities on matching it current and futures needs & profits.

<u>(Atrill, P. & McLaney, E)</u>

<u>Kamran Kashani, Robert Howard. (2013)</u>
<u>Erkki K. Laitinen. 2013)</u>Martin Lally, Steve Swidle(2008)
<u>Erkki K. Laitinen.(2006)</u>

<u>obert Ferstl, Alex Weissensteine(2011)</u>

Figur4.1

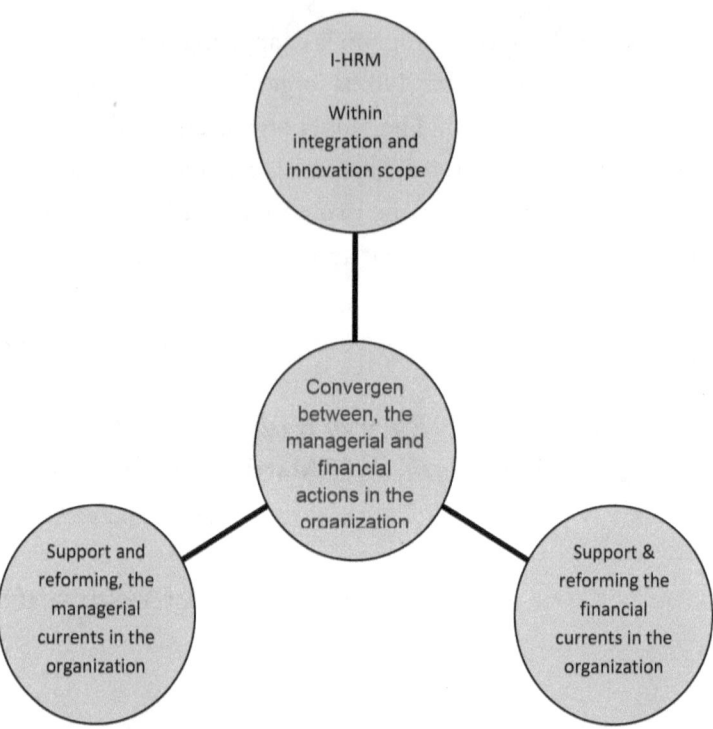

The above figure is showing the integration cycle from I-HRM of Nokia organization, especially in reflecting the HRM performance. In establishing and reforming some sections. Like: the IT section, financial section, managerial section, especially in introducing all of currents and futures plans for this organization, by sharing the financial and managerial actions in one current to achieve some important targets like:

1- Matching the Nokia productions with all of the domestics and international markets needs during decades of performance and integration.

2- Reforming the sales revenues for this Superior organization

3- Support the Permanently of the organization during the past and current decades.

For this issue, The I- HRM sector in this global organizations is passing, the good way, to reflect some positive actions, regarding, the organizations performance to reform the organizations, to match all targets and needs during the competitions journey with itself or with other organization in all of demotic and international markets. And how the HRM could expect, the organizations needs, especially in matching, the future requirements and needs, to avoid the occurring of any crises or dilemma, that could touch the soul of the organizations performance or targets. For this, the good understanding for the history of the HRM from the past decades till nowadays could support any one, who's interesting, in this management field, to take the juice, of I- HRM experiences and interactions with locals and international firms, experiences and actions and expecting for the talent currents and actions during this nice management field.

UNIT Five

THE I-HRM in Selection & Managing The Organizations Cultures

Abstract

Nowadays The superior international firms are trying to guide the multi nationals different staff with their different cultures and believes to support the goad values within the organizations culture norms, by respecting their values & improving their loyalty for their organizations values and targets within international firm norms. Thus, the organization management should recommending and select the best strategies and plans, to reform the international organization mechanisms in the integration currents.

Introduction

Initially, The best currents for Managing culture within venture or organization, will alliance the talents norms to support and push the integration trends during the business environment, for any firm or organization. Because the culture is the main source of ideas & believes during the business interactions. In a same way (**Barry**), was introduced his argument about this Issue, by saying that "The essence of capitals growth within some Asian nations are related for common cultural roots". For this, it will be so easy to understand that, the international firm or venture will get more opportunities for more integration norms, because of different nationalities within it environment. In a same way the Author (**Frank B**), was providing his argument about managing cultures advantages by saying that" The interaction between domestic culture and global operations was support the economic Norms in temporal context during some nations like US or Japan". Therefore, the HRM are passing in smooth and strong way, to draw a nice picture About the journey of managing the cultures scales for the organizations from the foundation, till interring the global markets and adding more values- talent actions for the organizations goals and targets.

The Concept of Organization Culture

Initially, the organization culture could be defined as; the environment for the staff or worker behaviors and mentalities within the organization environment boundaries. In the same way, it could be defined as, the norms of human's interaction or believes within their values and practice during their region.

For this, the individual's interactions during their region with common issues and behaviors could provide the ability to shape or reshape the individual's action and performance. Therefore, the HRM are focusing about the best managerial methods and practical frames, to reform the organizations goals and targets, by managing and arrange the best mechanisms to interact with the organization culture and guide the juice of these interactions to support the staff performance for their organizations. Even if they are performing in-out for their organizations boundaries. In the same way, the interaction between the staff behaviors and the venture or firm goals will reflect more integration and innovation within the businesses environment for the firm or venture. For this issue, the firm management should polish some tools & factors to support its targets. Like: beliefs, political systems, religion and technologies in the organization, by selecting and managing of some imperative factors during the organizations cultures. To achieve some important points for the organization during its demotic journey and reform the organization within its interactions with the modern global markets, needs and requirements. Like: managing the organization staff during their believes during flexible scope. Because, Normally almost individuals trying to select they're believes during their behaviors suppose if their believes Is positive or negative. For this case, Most of international managers are trying seriously to match the staff believes with organization activities or targets, by using a good level of communication skills to Introduce more opportunities for more comfortable working environment and avoid any conflict or dilemma in integration trends within organization. Therefore, the organization management should be aware regarding the soul of a political system in the organization because the political system is more able to provide all facilities to reflect the essence of national culture. In the same way, the political trend is running through tolerance and good relation currents, To provide more ability to control some serious issues. Like: economics interactions or relation between nations. In the same way, the organization management should reflect a strong respect for its Staff religions and believes. Because, the Religions are crucial source of ethics and values within any national culture, for example, Christian religion is focusing about the value of the business during human interactions. In the same way, the Islam religion deprived Alcohol. For this, the international manager should have more information about others culture to avoid any performance leakage during the organization activities. Finally, the international organization management should have some important skills to manage the wide scope of different mentalities and values. Like: negation skills and communications skills, to avoid any misunderstanding or miscommunication between staff or members during different cultures believe or values. In the same way, the organization management should focus in the strong way, to push the integration tools for the technologies in the organization. because the technology is able to provide the best ability & capability to passing all boundaries and different culture within a short time because of it modern facilities in communications for this the International manager need to match the level of technology with other culture needs

The Links between National Culture and the International Firm

Since last decades, the globalization norms were passing to change humans thinking and believing, during their national culture and others foreign cultures. In the same way, the globalization was laying flexible and strong currents for cross culture management and other similar action. For this case, the Author **(Chevrier)** Was introduce his argument, by saying t" the international managers should look for culture as a serious issue within the business environment Scales. In a same way the Author (Chevrier) was focusing about the important of national culture scales by saying that" the managers should focus about the national cultures norms even if it running during global norms". For example, Switzerland's citizens living dour national political culture norms Within Switzerland nations"

The Concepts of National Culture

Actually, the main observation for the political national culture is to push the mechanism for the essence of values rather than the frame of the values during culture norms, to laying a clear firm about the command issues between different mentalities & believes during one common culture. For this issue, it will be an easy issue to recommend that the political culture is able to introduce the best capability to transfer the national culture during globalization currents in a strong way to improve the international organizations for more integrations and achievements during it activities and goals.

Example 5.1

Switzerland culture

The Switzerland was established in 1848. In the same way it is classified as heterogeneous nation because of the roots for it citizens are from Italian, French and German with different religions like portents and catholic. In the same way, the Switzerland was divided during spirit regions and every region is having its special behaviors and mentalities which Mean internal boundaries within Switzerland nation. For this, every region within Switzerland Is have it special authority, government and education.

Switzerland during political culture Norms

Suppose the different of values & ethics within Switzerland nation. The Switzerland government is decide to guide all different trends in religions, langue's and behaviors during low & Legal currents, because The Switzerland government is believing, that the laws applying currents are able to distribute all integrations and innovation during comfortable & smooth environment. For This the Author, **(Chevrier)** was introduced his argument by saying that 'the common rules within Switzerland nation were laying a strong and safety frame within Switzerland and this safety could provide more capability to improve the Switzerland power.

National political Culture during Management Norms

The Switzerland lows and common regulations are showing a high level of safety &respectful working environment within Switzerland venture or firms. Because any one could recommend several useful issues which support any management during its activities. For example the working between males & females in a comfortable atmosphere, or solving any dilemma between workers or labors within any firm during conciliation atmospheres, because The Switzerland nation during it political national culture is trying seriously to making a good balance between the structure and structure applying within any demotic working environment. Finally the political national culture is passing to improve some nations like, Switzerland and support the management activities by guiding different individuals with their different languages, religions and values within common norms which protecting by rules and regulations to provide More flexibility and security for business integration by making balance between rules and rules By Applying during respecting and conciliation norms.

Chevrier (2009)

Values within organization

The values in the organizations, like the physicals and communications values between the organizations staff and the values between staff and organization, like cooperation –coordination, are classified as important tools within organization environment performance. For this issue, the management researchers are saying that, the values could provide strong tools within organization Environment mechanism during several actions or issues. Like: guiding decision between important or non important actions, values could provide more opportunities for the organization Members to introduce more achievements for the organization performance. Finally the values could change the organization actions or operations during managers actions, especially if the manager's values matching organization values, Therefore, the HRM in the organizations are support the scope of working environment within the organization is drawing the natural of interactions during the organization activities. In a same way, the businesses researchers recommend that, the positive environment is have the good ability to guide the staff interactions during positive way to support the influence current for the organization performance integration within the organization. Like: materials using or recycling. For this, the organizations managers should shape the organization environment during strong ethics & values to push the organization environment and attitude. In the same way, the growth of globalization norms during the organization, was improving the individual's interactions during ethics and values within organization environment. For this, the organization management is needed to guide it different staff with their different intents & behaviors during positive currents to provide more opportunities for it integrations & innovations norms, because any dilemma between staff or conflict between employees with their working environment will occur some crises within the Organization performance or making some dilemmas during integration scales within organization. For example," the WTO & UN organization are passing to supporting the ethical environment during global economic to push and support the global economic activities. For this, the organization management should introduce a fit current between values and organization environment."(**Hyo Sung**).

HRM within Global Culture

In this hybrid scope of implementations and competitions regarding the international organizations activities within global markets, The I-HRM are required to shaping the organization during its new mission by understanding others cultures. Especially if the organization is providing it activities during global trend. by lay a flexible frame to understand the different members – staff, during their multi behaviors & interactions to guide the different trends and actions during clear norm by doing some actions. Like: comparing between cultures during individuals interaction within the internal environment for the organization. In the same way, the organizations mangers, should deal with organization members & staff in the clear and honest trend and avoid any dilemma during staff interaction, by showing them the respecting for their culture. In the same way, the manger should avoid any forcing to other cultures by using good communication skills & negation. For this important issue, The Author **(Giorgos)** was said that "The organization manger should introduce and present a good example, for his personal values to other member and staff by showing all of the power and self respecting during his interaction to others. In the same way, the organization manager should reflect the loyalty for his job and show more respecting to others staff in the organization during his-her interactions with them and provide for them cooperation – support to push the organization staff performance during good level". Finally, the manager should provide and introduce the essence of integration & successful to others. 'For example, in Sweden nation the manager should have the Ability and capability to distribute power within the organization. On other hand, the I-HRM, are introducing some modern systems, to support their interactions mechanisms during the global culture for the organizations. For example, in the some superior's organization, the HRM are selecting a modern system wish named, (culture system), To manage the individual's interactions during their common environment issues. Like: mentalities, believes and customs. In The same way, the culture System could relate for the individuals made, during their environment to support and push their probability for their organizations. For example" The language could support the communication norms between individual's relations. For this, the language or other similar issues within human made culture could Support the human activities and push it during strong current within people interactions" **(Lane Kelly).** In the same way, the Author **(Chan-Hoong Leong)** was defining culture by saying that," Culture is the norms of human's interaction or believes within their value and practice within their region." For this the individual's interactions during their region with a common issue like behaviors- language, could provide the ability to shape or reshape the individual's behaviors.

Culture Norms within international Organizations

In fact, the implementation during global interactions between economic and social norms is introducing several integration currents within organization or nation achievements. For example "the successful history of peoples China Bank to remove British interest in 1997 is related to the bank dealing with political, social and economic tools within China norms "(Lane Kelly). For this, it will be an easy issue, to recommend that, the domestic's organizations interactions within social and economic currents could support the Nation integration during globalization activities. For this issue the Author (**Lane Kelly**). Was introduced his argument by saying that "the Organization should introduce and provide its best effort to push its rules within the highest efficiency level to support the organization mechanisms." Thus, the growth of globalization interactions likes Negotiation or other similar issue, to support and push the global business environment within nations,. Because the negotiation is supporting the atmosphere between two organization or more, by building conveyance and clear working frame between parties. Thus, The Author (**Lynn E Metcalf**) was introducing his argument for this issue by saying that" The organization need strong and flexible access gate to avoid any tendencies or Dilemma occurring during the scope of international organization activates". Finally, there are some Crises within organization values & ethics could make a serious leakage during the organization integration currents like, Collectivism, Opportunism and Individualism. For example, "The individualism staff is focusing about his need more than a group or organization needs". (**Chaco C Chen**).

Culture goes to Economic Integration

Indeed, The international cultures interactions within international firms environment, are introduced a flexible current to guide common behaviors or believes during easy scales of activities and performance. In the a same way, the improvement of education and technologies facilities like, mobiles, internet or other similar issue, was providing more opportunities to support the common currents within internationals cultures. For this, the cultures convergence could provide more opportunities for economic improvement. In the same way, the Author' (**Lane Kelly**). Was introduced his argument by saying that" the interaction between china and the West during last decades, was allowed to introduced common currents and convergence norms Between china and west." For this, it will be clear to Said that, the interactions between china and west could push the economic power within the two nations, because the business cultures convergence between China & West could push the negotiations or agreements forms during integration scope between China and West. In the same way, the Author **(Lane Kelly).** Was introduced the convergence tool with its activity to punch and support the economic integration, by saying that," the convergence between organization cultures, is used to collect cultures data during clear form and use it upon needs in static methods to provide more opportunities for culture changing to match the culture improvement needs like, changing positions or other similar issue during Hypothesis method or other method ". Thus, The essences of cultures convergence methods, are to provide more flexibility or opportunity to change Some values with cultures or some cultures to match some integrations targets. Suppose the humans in any culture are providing their interactions and believe during knit currents, especially with their religions, values and languages. For this the cross verging need to establish an acceptable norms during it trend without damaging other cultures knits by using some tools like, data collections, Because The data using, could provide benefits and advantages to support economic integration within Nations, by guiding all common values or ethics between cultures during common levels of organization environment. Like: management level within organization or organization activities.

Organization within global cultures interactions

Since last decades the improving globalization during manufacturing and marketing was an alliance to the global investments for organizations. For this issue, The organizations staff or employees need to deal with different individuals or managers with their different values and believes. For this, the guiding the interaction between different staff or management to different staff will be a difficult and complex issue. Thus, the organization culture should have the ability and capability to match the individuals within organization interactions, by guiding the different values & mentalities within clear norms between organization needs and staff needs. For this, the Authors, **(Catherine T Kwants, Chery A Boglarks)**, are defined the organization culture, by saying that' the organization culture is guiding the individual's values, interactions and behaviors during common targets and goals. In the same way, The Authors **(Richard Mead & Tim G.Andrews)** Are defined the organization culture by saying that, "the organization culture is the norms of rules within values and believes." On other hand, The Authors **(Catherine T Kwants, Chery A Boglarks)** are provide an argument about the important of organization culture, by saying that, the organization culture is providing the confidence norms during the employees interactions in a high level. For this, the organization should introduce it culture norms during clear and easy way to improve the perception ability for it culture norms between employees because the clear Understanding of the organization cultures norms, will sweep any conflict or misunderstanding within organization operations or interactions which improve the staff ability for more integration and avoid any weakness or crises within the organization goals and needs. For this, the Authors, **(Catherine T Kwants, Chery) A Boglarks)**, are provide an argument regarding this important issue by saying that, "The organizational culture could have the ability to push the organization outcomes". Finally the Authors **(Pallavia Srivastava & Jyotsna)** are provide another argument about the important for organizational culture, by saying that," The improving and increasing of fairness within US organizations, was reflecting more implementations norms within staff skills and this changing could be recommended during 500 firms in US". In a same way the Authors **(Catherine T Kwants, Chery)**, Are looking for national culture as an important part or tool within organization culture because the national culture is reflect the organization norms during langue, mentality and behavior within organization interactions and targets. For this, They are introducing their argument by saying that," The employees within the organization are trying to select their own methods or their previous experiences or information to the organization environment." For this, the Authors, **(Catherine T Kwants, Chery)**. Are present an argument by saying that "The staff in the organization are laying their experiences during their interactions within their organization norms." For example, the relationships between staff within US organizations are running during tolerated currents, but in the Japan it running during serious actions currents" In a same way the Authors, **(Richard Mead &**

Tim G.Andrews). Are showing some differences between organizational culture and national culture during some issues. like: the national culture is specific for one group during their beliefs and values, but the organizational culture could have more that different groups with different beliefs & values. The national culture could provide more flexibility for it believes or behaviors norms but in the organization culture need to guide different believes to match it needs or provide some forcing for others cultures to match it needs. Finally, the organizational culture could provide some norm during other processes like negation To support other culture activities within organization integration trends. For this **(Richard Mead & Tim G.Andrews).** Are explain the negation mechanism within organizations, by saying that," The negation is reflecting the management actions to support and improve the new strategy for the organization. Especially if the new strategy is able to push the integration scales within organization" Thus, the bottom of challenge during negation operations in the organization, is to provide some methods of changing and keep the organization under authority to avoid any conflict or dilemma within organization environment during the selecting of the new strategy or strategies, to support the loyalty between staff and organization and pushing the organization goals. On other way the Authors, **(Lynn E.Metcalf, Allan Bird, Mahesh Shankarmahesh,)** Are Locking for negation frame, by saying that, "supporting some relationships within some parties' and these Relationships could provide clear framework to support the integration between organizations or nations to push the outcomes recourses, by following some actions. Like: using the common cultures or values during negations '. For example, most Europe nations have some common values & behaviors which mean more opportunities for good negations and voiding any tendencies during negations to guide the negations into positives environment to draw a strong Frameworks within parties. Finally using the modern technologies materials could support the Negations interaction like using video conference.

Cross – cultural Team Mission

Actually the Cross-cultural team, are proposing a nice effort for an international organization performance, in managing the malty cultural techniques, because

The main mission of cross-cultural leadership. Is to introduce an active media and relationships within different cultures between managers and staff, wish reflecting some positive actions. Like: cooperative environment within the staff interactions, because the cooperative is a nice tool to push the cross cultural leader ship to the headway for the integration norms. In the same way, the cooperative is supporting the trust with staff interaction and the trust supporting the positive interactions and norms. For example," The Chinese are passing to cooperate and coordinate with Japanese leaders by supporting their common values during their interactions and relationships to support condense and trust currents during their actions". **(Chen, Dean Tjosvold)**. For this, The business relations between China and Japan, are common within similar values. wish make more comfortable norms between the Japanese leaders and Chinese staff interaction. Thus, the cross –cultural team is able to provide more integration performance and attitude, because they believe that,' Me and my manager are working to achieve some goals'. For this, the cross – cultural team are able to deal with real difference values and behaviors, because the ability of cross-cultural leadership to support the relationship between management and team, by supporting the theoretical understanding, by introducing some practical issues. Like: training. But in the same way the international cross –cultural team interactions could run during complex or conflict norms because of the some differences in communication, attitude, authority and proper decisions.. In the same way, the cross cultural team, are laying the best foundation to support their integration and performance, during their interactions in the international organizations, by introducing and acting some important currents. Like: Communication scope, Attitude and Authority, and the environment for an international culture in an international organization.

Communication scope

The communication within cross-cultural team should be clear and direct, to avoid any confused Or conflict within cross-cultural team communication even if they dealing by several languages or accident. Therefore, the leadership should ask to use one common language during their communication. In the same way, every culture is reflected it communication style within culture diversity interactions. For example, In the US Culture, the people are direct in speaking and asking clear question. in a same way the Japanese are using indirect questions and focusing about their emotions In a serious way. For example," When the Us Manager was presenting some data systems In Japanese firm. They recommend that, The Japanese staff was talking and discussing after that they decide what they could talk about during the organization actions". **(Brett, J., Behfar, K. & Kern, M.)** For this, any confused between direct and indirect communication could create some conflicts norms within firm outcomes or interactions.

Attitude and Authority Norms

The bottom of Challenge in cross-cultural leadership is to lay clear boundaries within the team interactions within the global organization, because of the different between the staff cultural values regarding the working attitude and authority. For example, the attitude in the hierarchical culture is mostly different in the egalitarian culture within the organization hierarchy cultural. Thus, the Authors **(Brett, J., Behfar, K. & Kern, M)**. Are introducing their argument regarding this issue, by saying that, "In The Mexican culture, anyone should design his question during form to show the humble for others even if he working as manager or normal staff".

Culture Scales During cross-cultural team

Actually the culture is very important issue in the organization interactions and cross - cultural team performance because it was modified during individual's behaviors and values. For this, the culture concept is could be defined as, the trend of solving the conflict within people. For this, the understanding of national cultures could support the cross-cultural team, to improve the international organization in its integration performance and it outcomes by supporting it cross- culture management and leaders, by supporting the management mission to guide the currents of different cultures to the international organization culture current during clear and flexible norms to match the cross-management team with international magnet, By laying a strong international culture to improve the organization ability and capability to manage the different behaviors and interactions within its environment. For example" some researchers in Europe culture are recommends that, Suppose the Europe culture is running during homogenization norms during it several organization cultures, the organization leaders are more familiar and comfortable to provide the successful interactions with different cultures because they are improve some international organization performance. Like: IBM Company" (**Brett, J., Behfar, K. & Kern, M.**)

Virtual Team

Because the Virtual Team is interacting and performing within different cultures and values, by using technology facilities, like Fax and email, to crossing the time in fast way to passing boundaries and nations to push the integration of organization. Therefore, they are forcing the HR performance to changing in meet their requirements during their interactions in coordination and cooperation within their organization. For this, the implementation of leadership is more complex during communication, job designing or description and training, to support the confidence norms between virtual team interactions. Thus, their main mission is to lead a virtual team to meet the global organization goals, by supporting the organization management trends and order within confidence and trust norms. For this, the HR trends within the virtual team should run with flexible currents to meet the huge scopes during virtual team, regarding working times, job descriptions and duties. Finally, they are required to introducing an active communication way to meet their different languages in one common media or language to avoid any confused or misunderstanding.

Conveying the international organization message

Initially in any sector, like marketing, banking and finance, the manager or team leader is like to convey his message or vision during clear way, to avoid any confused or misunderstanding because any misunderstanding within any message or conversation, could make a serious leakage within the message targets or needs during several issues. Like: decisions making, interactions and introducing some managerial actions. In the same way, The growth of globalization is guiding the manager to select his message within different cultures, values and languages. For this, The organization manager mission, is being more complex to match His –Her performance message with others staff, during their different languages & values and haw he could make the communication operation during sustainability current, to match the fast changing of mentalities or behaviors especially with lower commons values or languages during the global scales. For this, the Author **(Thomas)** was introducing some tools to support the scope of communication within international markets interactions, by saying that, "One of the important achievement for the organization management, is knowing the customers believes to match their believes with the production style, finding an easy or common language within markets environment. Finally, the organization management should look for the organization sustainability within markets, by expecting customers Emotions & values." For this it will be easy to recommend that, the essence of active consuming during global markets with its different culture is by making a good balance between the multicultural customer's needs, emotions and markets needs during active & clear communication. In the same way, **(Thomas)** was focusing about using the values within international communication scope, suppose the values changing fast because selecting common values with global communication interactions could be an active tool to match others needs during clears communications norms. For example, "From 1990, the central bank was recommending the importance of communication with citizens and investors, to have a clear idea about their expecting about very important financial operations. Like: interest rates, currency exchange values, by analysis their opinions and expectations in financial interactions, during the short future career In financial to improve the central bank a ability to draw a clear frame about future of financial interactions for this the central bank was giving more opportunities for citizens and investors, to express their emotions freely and provide for them flexible norms for any financial question or attention during speeches or other sessions with other international banks supporting like, Us bank." **(Matthias Neuenkirch.)** Finally the using of language during clear way could support the integration of international businesses interactions because clear language, will mean clear media in businesses operations and negotiation to designing a clear and strong business frame but there are some dilemmas during language practice or interactions during different languages. For this, the Author **(Jacques Melitz)** was providing the suggest in using the common language between different nations businesses, because the common language is more able to support foreign trading." For this, a common language is alliance the international business to run during flounce way between two nations and more. And reduce the expense of translators. For example, the using of English language as common langue between India & Tanzania.

The Strategies of Convergence between branches

Now days, the relationship between IHRM and MNC is running during the current of challenging, To meet the modern requirements and targets to provide more opportunities in international firms implementations during deal with the essences of cultures diversity, because the knowing Of different cultures is very active tool to match others cultures and information with international Organizations needs and targets, Wish support the integration of international organization, because the information is a good media to introduce the best sharing and interactions between others needs and behaviors. For this, the social capital could be defined as the" increasing of information during international markets environment. For this, it will be easy to recommend that, the social capitals are supporting the IHRM to passing all boundaries and cultures, to make the IHRM mission easier during their Cooperation & coordination in the global markets and organizations. In the same way, the using of modern technology could be an active tool during IHRM activities with social capitals.

Like: using internet, because the modern technologies is keeping the IRHM in touch to recommend others information and need and analysis some actions or behaviors to expecting the future need for global customers and markets, especially with high values boundaries and markets. For this,(**Taylor**) was introducing four steps to build an active social capital during the integration of dealing with different of values and behaviors, especially in knowing the legal environment within host nations regarding some important issues. Like: labors wages, currency exchange rate and value and requirements or conditions for investments within the host nation for the investment. In a same way, the national culture is the important cell during global interactions because the national culture could introduce the norms of other cultures accepting and supporting during the national culture individualism in their actions and behaviors during their experience and behaviors. Finally, the tolerance is very useful Issue within social capital because intolerance the IHRM will guide their power in positive issues. Like: introducing new rules, performance plans and actions within others cultures. Thus, the organization management should avoid any conflicting within cultures, because the power will be running in negatives issue, which occur some leakage in social capitals trends. In a same way the trust during social capitals could provide Comfortable interaction during polishing the relationship between culture and others cultures, because the trust is distribute confidence norms between parties and support others acceptance especially with different cultures during sharing data and experiences. In the same way, any misunderstanding between cultures could occur some conflict or dilemma between the different cultures integration because of missing trust.

Example 5.2

In 1976, the German bank was planning to establish a new branch in Bangladesh nation, to provide more opportunities for more financial interaction and providing loans for locals investments. Like: Agriculture and manufacturing sectors, to refresh the domestics economic of Bangladesh and to take the benefits of financial transactions and loans interest benefits. Especially the Bangladesh is still emerging country and announced for its independence in 1971. For this, 'Mohammed Younus' the manager of this project, was starting to lay clear boundaries to introduce more acceptance and opportunities for this investment, by providing flexible loans for agriculture investments, which guide the Bangladesh center bank to provide more supporting for this foreign investment. For this achieving, the German bank was establishing a new branch on 1983, and this branch was limited in the agriculture sector in Bangladesh. In a same way' Mohamed Younus' Was passing to lay the trust norms for this bank, by taking the benefit of his teaching experience to persuade Some locals about the advantages of constitutions loan from German bank. Thus 'Mohamed' was passing again to alliance the locals farmers for the German bank epically by helping the poor locals For some loans with limit granite that support the respecting norms of German bank within Bangladesh citizens. Finally, Mohamed was providing some vacancies for some locals in German Bank, to support the social interactions during the banking environment.

(Asif Dowla, 2006).

Therefore, the (I-HRM) for the international organizations, are aware regarding the modern contemporary organizations needs and requirements during the good understanding for the essence of cultural globalization interactions in the organizations, because in the international organizations, every individual within international organization is reflecting his national culture with it values and behaviors during his-her working performance, interaction and communication. For this, the successful manager is trying seriously to know will about others cultures, to make a good balance between others cultures acceptance, to provide more motivation and integration within organization and shape others cultures and values during the international organization culture and values to support the international organization outcomes & objectives, by shaping some requirements and needs within international organization. Like: matching the management expecting during the staff performance, providing good quality within performance integration and introducing good attitude – communication within working interactions. In a same way, The Author **(Ralston, D.A)**, was interdicting an three important tools for Convergence, convergence and divergence within organizations, to provide more integration during the cross-cultures values interactions, buy select the understanding and using of the individuals behaviors and values to create the values evolution, during strong scales to match motivation or other similar issue, For this the convergence is reflecting the smart values of the interactions between the social culture and the business mechanism during this culture. In the same way the deep understanding Of some issues like, when & where the values should changing because the best selecting for smart values, could provide more opportunities For more integration within convergence norms within organizations. In a same way the Convergence is alliance for using The technologist issues to support the values changing to laying some acceptance for the business interacting within them social culture, because the using of modern technologies will improve The individuals information which improve their ability to understanding the benefits of changing or updating some social values to fit some businesses. Finally, the Divergence is guiding the individuals to interact directly with their social culture scope which mean providing more fluency for their social culture during the interactions with economic or political changing

Example 5.3

In China, especially the Hong Kong region, it will be an easy issue to recommend the general concept o convergence of performance management, because Hong Kong was passing to deal with three currents. The Current 1 is providing the flexibility and influences within china social culture. The Current 2 is interacting in a good way within UK Business. suppose the different values and behaviors between China and UK. The Current 3 is reflecting the integration of commerce operations between china and west suppose there are some gaps between china culture and West culture during values and behaviors.

(Ralston, D.A.)

Headquarters and subsidiary

On other hand, The authors **(Richard Mead & Tim G.Andrews)**. Are recommending the relationship between headquarters and subsidiary within interactions during some issues. Like: culture, HRM and technology within norms of controlling and risk especially cultural risk. Especially when The Headquarter is trying to force the national culture within subsidiary foreign culture norms which Occur some conflict or leakage performance, because of missing motivation or trust between the subsidiary and headquarters. For this the management within Headquarter should providing more Opportunities and flexibility within their interactions with subsidiary, by laying a clear frame of Tolerance norms during the interacting between subsidiary and the foreign culture and providing a clear mechanism to push and support the common advantages between the national culture of headquarters and foreign culture of subsidiary. For Example, "The Coca-Cola firm is very famous organization because it consume it product during global markets, which it Headquarter in UK and its subsidiary branches in others regions, but in 1999 this global firm was surfing from dilemmas to falling during it international activities. For this the new CEO Douglas who is making anew restructuring the organization by sweeping 6000 staff during the main Branch and some others branches, to support the balance between the national culture of Coca-Cola main branch and foreign cultures for some international branches. For this in 2000. the Cola Company was drawing its integration from UK to Arabian Gulf".(**Richard Mead & Tim G.Andrews**).

Conclusion
Ericson & China
Negotiation with China

Initially, any business negotiation should be running with some prior interactions, to laying business agreement during the frame of clear rules to managing the different behaviors and values during the practical actions between the different parties. In the same, the negotiation, especially the international negotiation with some nations like. China should be running during three important managerial steps. The first step is pre- negotiation. The second step is negotiation. The third step is post negotiation.

Negotiation between Ericson & China

Actually, The telecommunication project between Ericsson firm and China domestics markets was a result of successful negotiation between Ericsson and China during the applying of three negotiation tools

1- Pre-negotiation

In this important step the China was using some basics arrangements, before any action or agreement. Like: the China used its government as the neutral party to submit all official conditions before any starting actions. Like: The availability of technological issues and martial to match the project needs. the ability of transferring the materials and equipments during the proper time Finally providing common and flexible norms between Ericsson and China to improve the ability of selling and interactions within china for the telecommunication project productions, by following some actions. Like: Lobbying: in lobbying the foreign investors should persuade some government sectors. Like: the ministries about the firm ability during it superiors productions and modern technologies facility, because the Chinese believe that, their integration during the foreign investment should be on the top. For this, the Ericsson was passing to persuade the ministry of communication in China about it modern communication materials. Presentation: the main target of presentation is to intruding the full information from the foreign firm to Chinese parents to informing them about the modern facilities for the foreign firm and it is productions quality & price to introduce a strong step for the negotiation between foreign firm and Chinese because of the data capitals from other firm and Chinese parents for this the Ericson firm was introduced a strong presentation about it activities and modern facilities but with some Mistakes like, using the English language during the presentation suppose the Chinese are not familiar with this languages and the number of translators are not more enough to match the Chinese audiences which occurring some gaps Within the presentation information. Trust building: generally the trust is guiding for motivation and builds a strong contraction of good relationships between the business parties For this the Swedish managers of Ericson organization are visiting china several times to know will about the Chinese values and behaviors and they are inviting the Chinese parents to their nation and the Ericson head branch To showing them their life and the modern facilities-technologies issues and sharing with them Some social activities to provide more trust and comfortable norms For this the Ericson management are discovering some leakage pointes in this investments like, some conflict within Chinese management and the lack of foreign currency exchange in china.

2- Formal Negotiation

The formal negotiation was starting seriously when the two parties are ready the Ericson management and the Chinese partners, by using the Bank of China as third party to do the official negotiation and laying the rules and conditions for the financial interactions and legal decimations agreements. For this, the negotiations parties are enjoying their negotiation during some several common tasks. Like: (Equity sharing management control, technologies issues, payment and price). Equity sharing: in the equity sharing the Chinese are laying a clear frame about their equity Sharing by make it 50%, because they are looking for the power within this project in activities and us it within some political interactions. Management Control: In this issue the Swedish are planning, to provide Training for the Chinese within the modern management operations. In The same way, the Chinese are looking for high positions within this foreign investment. For this, the Ericson management is appointing some their staff management in high positions, to provide training to Chinese staff and allow For Chinese in others high positions. Like: HRM. Technology: the negotiation about technology was focusing about willingness of technologies issue between Ericson and China, because the Chinese believe that, when they are submitting the agreement they will have the rights to takes all the benefits from the Ericson technologies. In the same way, the Ericson management is worried about the protection of its technologies materials.

3-Post Negotiation

Indeed, the post negotiation sector in Ericson, was recommending some errors within the negotiation operation between Ericson and china. For example, when Ericson was selecting it direct manger within this project regarding the agreement between it and china the direct manger they were facing some conflicts issues and misunderstanding during some actions and cases. Like: the conflict between West and china within some standers and values during the interactions between the Swedish manager director and the Chinese senior executives. in the same way, the salary of Swedish director is more than the salaries of 200 Chinese staff. For this case the Swedish are asking Chinese to making anew negotiation solve this dilemma.

(Ghauri, P. & Fang, T.)

UNIT Six

THE HRM in Selection & Managing The Organization Performance

Introduction

Before some decades, The HRM researchers are locking for the business performance within any Organization management during narrow scales because they are thought that, the performance management is only focusing about some documentation and actions. Like: surveys, evaluation and training. However, they don't know will about the gaps between the surveys and management performance. However, this topic was changing during our modern contemporary, because of using modern technology facilities. Like: computers- internet. Therefore, the business Researchers are recommending that, the training or survey is a part of management performance, because every superior organization is trying seriously to do it best in improving & supporting the job performance for its staff and employees during it working environment, by using modern computers or systems for this mission, because of it highly quality and the economic price. For this, the improving staff performance during the organization activities, will reshaping the organization interactions and performance in positive trends & push the organization to the integration current to meet its targets and needs. For Example," in 1978 the management of peoples bank of china (PBC) are passing to support the internal financial interactions by introducing some modern systems and rules to reforming the level of internal bank system and giving the loans opportunities for houses owners to refresh the locals stocks".(**Fu, Shelagh Heffernan**)

The concepts of performance Management

Initially, the management performance is could be defined as, some practical methods or techniques to manage the Organization workers during some processes and actions, to support the staff performance within the organization. In a same way, the Author (**Aguinis, H**), was defining the management performance, by saying that," The management performance is important tool within organization mechanism, because it providing some processes and operations to improve and support the organization staff or teams, to Improve the organization ability to meet its goals, with some components. like, continuously in some operations like, protecting, guiding and goals achievements. For this, the Authors, (**Yu-Shan Chen, Ming-Ji James Lin, Ching-Hsun Chang**), **A**re providing an argument regarding this important issue, by saying that, "The innovation of management performance within organization could provide several advantages during the organization relationships and capacity, especially in support the organization achievements and goals."

Performance management within Technologies Scales

Initially, the capital of any organization is the humans. For this, the superior HRM within the modern organization is selecting the modern technologies issues. Like: computers, networking and modern systems. Like: (distribution management system), to take some benefits during humans interactions within organization norms. Thus, the HRM within organization are required to guide the humans skills and experiences during the integration current to meet the organization targets and needs, by discovering the weakness operations during the staff performance and introducing the solutions to support the quality trend during practical way, by establishing a proper case for the new system to recommending and discovering the methods of new strategies during the system. Like: rating performance system for staff and providing some ideas or planning to improve the staff performance within the organization. Like: training or other similar issue, to support the organization profits and goals.

For example," In 2003 the management of people's bank of china (PBC), are introduction anew commissions system for local banking sector to reform the banks staff performance during financial operations and supervising the cash flow interactions during domestics markets of China". **(Fu, Shelagh Heffernan.)** For this, we could recommend that, the networking Performance is a good tool to guide the organization objectives and targets within one flexible current, because its providing all of positive interactions, actions and solutions within the organization by building a qualified staff or team, providing some practical planning for more integration, support the comfortable atmospheres within working environment in the organization, especially between managers and staff and providing a clear summary to reflecting the performance level for the organization staff.

The Recommending

On my opinion, I could be Said that, the workers behaviors during their performance interactions are reflecting their values or information during the organization scope. For this, any conflict or leakage during the values or information within any organization, especially the international organization, because of it cultural diversity will occur some crises or dilemmas during the organization targets and needs or some others important actions. For example, but not in limited, goals setting, decision-making action actions. In The same way, if the values and information are running through flexible and strong performance currents, the performance of the organization will run during the integration trend, especially by using some of the performance management processes. Like: planning or assessment. Because, the proper planning or assessment will polish the performance essence within organization, by reshaping it performance scale. For this important issue, the organization management requires to lay a strong & clear frame around the Performance management system in several tasks. Like: recommending, establishing, providing planning & solutions and Support the solution during talents activities. Therefore, the HRM, should recommending the importance of the performance management during the performance mechanism environment within the firm or organization, because the performance management, will provide a The performance of the business is an integrated and continuous contrary to some other issues such as valuation, which affects the sustainability of efficiency in raising the professionalism during the levels of constant & suspicion within the organization Performance. In the same way, the Author, **(Aguinis, H.)** was introducing his argument regarding this issue, by saying that" Initially, the appraisal is occurring once time during the year without feedback interactions. In the same way, the performance management is forsaking about the improving & supporting the positive interactions between the staff and management during several issues. Like: cooperation or sharing the performance feedback within comfortable atmospheres". For this I could said that, if the organization is believing seriously about the performance management advantages to growth its staff performance & interactions, it will be ready to Interacted in strong & flexible way to lay the basics issues for performance management system during the organization environment. In the same way, the performance management system is more able to sweeping any conflict or dilemma during this interaction. Wish guide the organization within integration norms, by improving the performance mechanism within the organization to improve it ability and capability to match it needs and targets. For example "In 1990, the U.S privet banking sector, was selecting the WMP system which mean: wealth management performance, to integrate the banks operations during some financial issues. Like: financial counseling & insurance issues to sweep the disadvantages of normal dealership, by providing more trust and comfortable norms during the financial interactions". **(Cheng-Ru Wu, Chin-Tsai Lin, Pei-Hsuan Tsai)**

Matching performance management process within organization needs

Indeed, the Sustainability of development and performance is one of the most important attributes of the performance management currents in the organization, even if the performance management is running within traditionally or advanced scales, especially within the staff performance within integration & implementation norms. For this, the organization should select it needs during the performance management. Like: mission and targets, to allowing for the performance management to introduce the professionals operations, to achieving the organization targets. For example, the using the staff reports or evaluations from the crossing management team, Like: Assistants or supervisors to recommending the commons issues with the staff Performance. like Information leakages or misunderstanding within some duties. In other example, "In U.K The Electronic Data Interchange Organization was planning to introduce a new system to support it actions and strategies planning during it businesses needs during UK markets. For this, In 1980 the EDI organization was passing to introduce the ISSP system which mean: Information system strategic planning and this new system was providing several advantages within it performance, especially by making a balance during it needs between information technologies and management issues to support it performance during UK domestics markets".(**John M. Ward**)

Crucible Performance Management within Organization Behaviors

Actually, The main aim of this managerial trend within some organizations, is to support the homogenization and synergy between the performance management and the organization within some specific performance mechanism, to push the innovation of staff reforming during some issues. Like: social power, trust, social change and negotiation, because the performance management is ready to avoid any tinkering issues. Like: performance actions or solutions during any operation in the staff performance, by enhancing the integration for the staff performance within their organizations, by selecting some actions. Like: social power and mentorship within organization interactions, wish support the organization needs. For this, the Authors (**Jamie A. Grumman, Alan M. Saks**). are providing an argument regarding this subject, by saying that" In the performance management, the negotiation between staff and organization during some actions. Like: goals seating or other similar issue, should Run during flexible current, by introducing some opportunities for the employee To express his-her feeling about the organization goals and targets. Which mean: To guide him-her for the organization goals engagement. On other hand, the organization management, should persuade him-her not to dissuade him, because the persuading of Staff or workers within the organization goals and advantages during the operations of selecting, planning and feedback, to guide the staff performance during positives advantages.

Appraisal Scope in Organization performance

Gnarly, the appraisal is using to evaluate the staff performance within the organization, even if their performance is bad or professional, to recommend any weakness aria or mismatching within staff performance and organization needs or targets. Wish improve it and support the staff loyalty within their organization performance, to push the organization behaviors within it goals and targets, but the case of (NPAS) in Malaysia, which mean. the new performance and appraisal system. Is mostly different and complex, because this appraisal is founding to guide the Malaysian teachers with their different trend and roots. Like. India or china nations within the appraisal current, to recommends their performance and feedback. Thus, this modern appraisal is able to avoid any cultural conflict within the organization because everyone is reflecting his-her culture and value during the business performance interaction within the organization. For this issue, the (NPAS), Is help The Malaysian government to convey for it staffs their appraisals result and the improvement planning, without any direct touch for their personals attitude and needs. Because if the teachers are receiving their appraisal directly or face to face they will provide the best action in this case like, performing in negative way or ignoring the organization needs." **(Rahman, S. A.)**

The NPAS disadvantages during the Foundation

From 1993 the Malaysian government was laying the NPAS during the rewards systems (Saran system) and WP&R system, which mean "Witnessed the beginning of formal system", to set the organizations outcome suppose the diffident cultures and roots in Malaysia nations, especially within the teachers activities and performance, by applying the essence of NPAS activities within flexible and comfortable norms. Like, open discussion or other similar issue between the top management and staff within the organization environment performance, To draw some goals during this interactions, but this trend of negotiation will make some conflict between staff and management, especially within large 'power distance' because It is difficult to manage the several interactions, values and goals setting within one managerial performance current. In a same way, In the 1997 the teachers are expressing their resentment about the NPAS regarding some actions. like; setting goals or objectives, because they believe that, ability and NPAS targets, to support the organizations targets and out comings. For those issues, the NPAS was present during 4 Hypothesis to interacting in good way during the matching the crossing culture with appraisal system, to push the integration of different teachers' performance and recommending the best Hypothesis during the best comfortable interactions and goals matching., they should setting the goals not The NPAS, because of their qualification and experiences. For this, their performance was running during down currents that occur mismatching between staff regarding their motivation.

The NPAS Hypothesis interactions

Hypothesis one

During this hypothesis., the teachers with their different roots and values will express the Missing points or links during the NPAS mission in reforming and supporting.

Hypothesis Two

During this hypothesis, the common issue is focusing about the ability of native Malaysian to carry on the NPAS teaching methods

Hypothesis Three

During this hypothesis, the teachers with high grade within evaluations and teachers with low level of evaluation but with clear feedback and guiding will get more opportunities for more comfortable atmospheres within high positions

Hypothesis Four

During this hypothesis, the teachers who are matching the NPAS conditions and requirements will provide more ability to carry on their duties.

The Common Issues

Actually, The NPAS participation is holding with 232 teachers, 29 teachers from India, 68 teachers from China and 135 teachers from Malaysia. For this, the questioners were started during six sections and levels. For example, the section one is focusing about understanding the system and section two is focusing about improving the system, etc,. during some flexible shape, to match the different values with this evaluation with confidentiality norms. For this action, the computerized result showing that there is 30% of the analysis volunteers are providing their Opinions and performance in neutral way. Thus, the hypotheses (1) was rejected because of the collectivism interactions during this evaluation, which mean the difficulty to applying the integration of teachers performance during their collectivism. In a same way the hypotheses Number (3) was founding a good environment within Malaysian teachers responding and interaction suppose their different roots and behaviors, because the essence of this hypotheses Is to introduce the discussion, feedback and responding during neutral norms during this appraisal, Which mean to focusing about the information and skills for the teachers more than their attitudes to avoided any direct interactions or conflict, because the direct interactions during the Appraisal will guide the teachers in positives performance norms, especially if the appraisal hypotheses is not matching their different believes or values which mean a serious leakage During any improvement planning or goals settings.

Strategic planning during Concept

Initially, the performance strategic plans are able to provide the best mechanism for the organization performance in several issues. Like: supporting the organization vision, mission and goals. Therefore, it is the best strategies to achieving the organization mission, especially if the strategic planning is using within performance management norms, because the performance management is focusing about two important points within organization performance. The first point is quality and the second point is continually. In the quality the performance management is support the strategic planning about the staff information and behaviors and in continually the performance management is focusing about improving the staff skills and ability to manage their Duties in nice way by providing some actions. Like: motivation and appraisals. In the same way, the actions should be continually during it interactions, to take the integration benefits within organization in long terms and targets, especially when the strategic planning is push the organization to convey it mission for several customers with their different values and behaviors.

Strategic planning during Concept and practical methods

Initially the performance strategic plans, are founding to provide the best mechanism for the organization performance in several issues. Like: supporting the organization vision, mission, Goals. In the same way, these strategies missions are able to achieving the organization mission especially if the strategic planning is using within performance management norms, because the performance management is focusing about two important points within organization performance. The first point is the quality, and the second point is continual. In the quality, the performance management support the strategic planning about the staff information and behaviors. in the same way, in continually the performance management is focusing about improving the staff skills and ability to manage their Duties in a nice way, by providing some actions. Like: motivation and appraisals, but those actions should be continually during it interactions within organization environment, to take the integration benefits within organization targets in long terms, Especially if the strategic planning is push the organization to convey it mission for several customers with their different values and behaviors. Therefore, this strategy is focusing in the strong way, to lay a strong construction of goals setting, analyzing the situation, consideration and implementation for the organizations. In the same way, the strategic planning is should running throw performance management norms for more continually and integration during some actions within strategic planning. Like: setting goals or case analysis. For this, the Author,**(Tapinos, E*)**. was introduce his argument about the advantages of performance management in improvement the measurement of strategic planning performance in the organizations, by saying that, "The relationship between strategic planning and performance management is running through integration current, because the performance management is able to improve The goad understanding the proper level of the performance management measurement during some actions". Thus, the relationship between strategic planning and performance management is able to introducing the best links during actives resources, monitoring the important objectives or targets. Like: improving the organization mission, making evaluations for management performance to improve the management skills and performance work interactions and supporting all issues about the information, technology availability within the performance current, For example, "The management of R&D organization was recommending some conflicts During their information about the competitors organizations and the real activities of this organizations. For this, the R&D organization was focusing about the technologies usage during two currents. The first current is to improve the technologies facilities in the organization and the second current is adding more technologies positions to take more continually benefits during the information interactions, to provide for R&D organization more opportunities in managing information to support their analysis and planning to push the R&D organization outcomes."**(Holger Ernst)**. For this I could said that, The management of R&D organization was using two currents in this case, The first current is to used the strategic analysis during implantation scope, by recommending the information conflict during it competitor with other organization and the second Current is to using the modern technologies and introducing technologies positions to support the R&D performance integration in analyzing information and providing planning& solutions in continually operations to improve R&D organization during it implantation & outcomes by polishing the essence of R&D mission during the Sustainability framework for it efficient work.

Common currents in organization performance

Indeed the strategic planning is running during performance management, to support the organization improvement in some management operations. Like: selecting the proper strategy, or staff appraisal, data analyzing or other similar issue to support the organization improvement for this, the understanding and analyzing of those tools will be very useful issue To support the understanding the development organization mechanism in continually scope. For example, In the appraisal operation. The evaluation of organization strategy is focusing about pushing the organization achievement during the organization improvement and planning. For this, it will be easy to recommend that, the performance of strategic planning is interacting with the organization environment within several issues. Like: working quality, staff performance and knowledge while laying and improving, by providing the best planning and leakage solutions to support the organization targets and needs.

Supporting the Performance Management System

Indeed, the improving and supporting the norms of performance management system within the organization, need some important tools. Like: the understanding of the performance system mechanism within the scope of activities and benefits. For this, The organization HRM should improve the scale of the smart understanding for the performance management system, to the biggest layer in the organization. Like: Management, staff and labors, To provide for them more opportunities regarding the interacting with this system, to discussed their opinion to what to do during this performance system and how this system could be more better. For this, the good arranging of the communication operation between the management and staff in the organization about the interactions and advantages of the performance system in organization, will provide more integration for the organization during the management performance system interaction to improve the organization ability and to meet it targets and needs.

The mechanism of Communication Plan

Actually the communication plan, should run during the performance management system. Thus, the mains issues and actions in the communication plane should support the Justice and clear information during the important interactions and questions. Like: what is the performance management? did the performance management match the organization strategy? Also, how the performance management is working within an organization? For this, I could Said that, a successful communication planning for performance management system should be running through clears process and actions. Like: guiding the different mentality and values during knowledge norms, especially for the management performance system advantages within organization. In the same way, The organization management should improving the performance level of organization and support the organization to meet its targets and needs. Thus, any misunderstanding or misinformation during the advantages of performance management, will cause some dilemmas or crises during the implementation of performance management system and in selecting the communication planning to push the implementation of performance management. For example, if some staff in the organization still thought about the performance management As a tool for deduction and warning he-she will never provide an highly loyalty for his organization and support the mechanism of the performance management interactions acceptance during his-her duties.

For this, the selecting of communication operation to support the performance management system needs for some more smart actions. Like: support the organization staff in establishing the new system, ask the organization staff about their needs, build a strong constriction about the performance system, By showing the system advantages and support this advantages with touchable evidences or proves, selecting the new system in neutral way, especially within international organization, because of different values and information finally using the talents of HR in selecting this issue Because they are in trust scope in interacting with management performance system and addressing the staff needs and requirements to select the understanding the performance management system in the organization.

Training advantages within performance management system

Initially, the training is very important tool within organization performance. Therefore, the organization HHR, are select the integration of performance management system during the organization, especially if the training is have the ability to improve the staff performance and behaviors to match it with organization performance and values because. Thus, the training is supporting several issues within organization trend during it journey with the performance management system. like: recommending the rezones of performance management integration, providing The proper information about the evaluations to introduce a performance management during smart Mechanism, reducing any errors during performance management system selection. like:supervisors, error in decisions making or other similar issues. in the same way, the training is bushing the staff performance within organization activities, by making appraisal for staff to prepare the proper plan to improve the staff information about the job scales. Like: duties and disruption. Finally, the training support the performance management system by increasing the self-motivation and good believes, by analysis the beliefs to support the positives advantages for Performance management interactions with staff within organization environment.

Team Needs within International organization

Because of international business Innovation and implementations, every organization are using the integration of team works within their organizations performance, To support several reasons. Like: support the organization ability for more performance in manufacturing and productions, reducing the numbers of hierarchical staff in an organization. Finally, the team is famous in fast responding during the works actions. In the same way, the team is defined as the two individuals or more working to gathers to achieving some goals and targets but may be in different areas interactions. Like: programming team from Canada insulting some software in UK. In the same way, the team is able for more internal managing to achieving the organization goals. finally, the organizations should manage the performance of the teams and Persons within its activities. For example, because of improvement of R&D organization during the global implementation. The R&D organization is managing its activities during the Teams working performance. "**(Jan Kratzer)** For this, the R&D teams are reaching virtual team level which reflecting the ability of R&D organization team to provide a good communication skills and coordination currents issues. Like: understanding their duties and organization targets to support the organization during clear communications scales and arrange the performance for the team during the good work coordination within the team interactions within their duties. Finally, the organization should measure the team performance, to push it integration by understanding the essence of the team during their duties, interactions and targets because the good understanding for the organizations team, will support the performance measurement to lay The proper tools to push the team performance to push the organization targets and needs.

Team's types

In this important issue, the HRM for the organization, are fully in charged to introduce the system performance for the organization team within acceptable norms, within clear performance, ethics and working interactions to support the organization needs and targets. For this, the organizations teams are classified regarding their duties a performance and expecting time for working within several groups. Like: project team, services team and network teams.

Services Team

In this team, the individuals in the organizations are common in the same skills or information and behaviors. In the same way, they are working in productions or manufacturing sectors for specific requirements and times.

Network team

This team is working within open norms of performance, which mean: out the organization because the network team is communicate during the modern technologies materials. Like: internet and their duties are related for counseling, to support the organization staff and performance.

Designing the team performance

Actually, The HRM is select some basics and requirements during the team selections in the organization, by fowling some steps. Like: insuring about the team ability to work During the organization regarding their numbers, qualifications and the team duties to match the team performance with organization objectives, by introduce a goad and clear communications skills, to explain for the team the proper information regarding their interactions with organization targets. In the same way, the organization HRM are required to measure the team effort within the organization to recommend any missing or gap between team performance and organization targets during several actions. Like: evaluation or open discussions. Finally, the organization HRM is required to focusing in the serious way regarding some actions within an organization. like: team behaviors and interactions, to support the organization ability to manage the performance system during flexible and clear currents.

Example 6.1

The' MySQL' is an international organization. Wish introduces a wonderful effort to manage its team's performance, suppose the complex norms during the organization performance and duties. Like: organization activities in arranging and entering the database and it international teams, which mean different information, values and behaviors. Thus, the HRM of the 'MySQL'. Are introducing open discussions and face to face interactions, to manage it teams performance. In the same way, the HRM of this international organization is introducing the clear information about the team's duties and comfortable working environment, by using the technologies facilities during communications and interactions.

(Jan Kratzer*)

Coaching Within International Organization

Initially, the coaching in the organization is very important issue during the organization performance management system, because the coaching is focusing about some important managerial currents within organization performance and activities, to push the organization to meet it targets and goals. Like: support the short performance interactions in the organization, which mean: the organization manager need to follow and support some daily operations within his-her interactions with the organization employees. For this, the HRM is applying and guiding the staff motivating to push the integration norms of staff performance. In the same way, I'd like To Said that, the clever manager should be able to interact in good way with guiding and motivation within employees working interacting, because in motivation the manager could remove any conflict between the staff and duties. In The same way, the manager will guide the staff performance to match the organization mission. For this, the organization manager should select the Best communications skills to guide the staff performance within organization targets. In the same way, the coaching could support the organization performance during some long targets. Like: supporting the organization improvement and the staff relationships within the organization, because the relationship between the staff and management with staff is very important tool to control the performance and avoid any occurring for any performance dilemma. In the same way, the coaching targets within organization performance, is to lay a goad frame of some important operations in the organization. Like: improving the employee's behaviors and providing the feedback for organization management. For this, I could Said that, the superior organization could support it long terms, by building a strong constriction For organization performance. Thus, the laying the strong basics of trust and good relationship, will improve the staff ability to introduce their performance during strong links to passing some complex issues. Like: cultural diversity between staff especially in international organizations. Finally the Authors **(Roger D. Evered, James C. Selman)**, Are defining the Coaching by saying that, "The coaching is support the performance improvement during guide the employees within specifics activities to support the organization activities and performance".

Coaching requirements

Actually The important issues in coaching, is to provide a good relationship between coach and employs to support the coaching trend in pushing the organization performance. For this, the coach in the organization is required to interact with good communication skills with staff to understand their needs and behaviors, to find the proper current to coaching the organization staff. In the same way, the coach is required to aspect any positives goals while coaching and believing will that, the coaching is an important tool in the organization during his-her performance and interactions. For this, the coach needs to make sure that; all staff understand their jobs needs and organizations tools. Finally the coach should Carry his responsibilities in serious way, because he- she is the source of coaching and his-her integration during this issue, will push the staff performance, which mean improving the organization ability to meet it targets. Therefore, The Coaching styles in the international organizations are classified regarding, attitude and performance in coaching the organization to Driver, persuaders, amiable and analysis operations in the organization. Thus, the smart coach is who could able to use those characters as masks during his coaching within staff. for example the coach in customer services should used the assertive mask in a same way in coaching of selling the coach could used the persuading mask to improve the marketing staff in persuading customers for some productions or items for this the coach should match between the attitude and coaching style during the coaching operation to introduce more advantages issues in improving the employees Performance within their organization. Thus, If I'm the coach for any organization, I will try to introduce my best effort, to improve the organization staff regarding their communication and I will try to select The four characters during the communication coaching operations. The first by using the persuading style to persuade the managers of this organization about the communication skills, benefits in the organization performance. Second I will use the assertive style to introduce the coach operation in fair and clear way. The third I will be amiable during the communication interactions during the coaching to improve the manager's motivations during this issue. Finally, I will be an analytical during my actions and feedback about the Coaching performance especially in matching the organization needs and targets.

The proper selections for Contingent Plane

For this important issue, the organization management needs to lay some flexible currents to select the contingent payment, to takes more benefits and advantages for it performance integration and implementation, by following some actions. Like: pace of rate. In this plane, the paying is reflecting the quality and the quantity of staff performance during some positions. Like: call center or reception. For the example, the quantity or the quality of calls or other operations during the interacting with clients especially in industrials sectors. Like: marketing sectors, because the employees in marketing, are taking more benefits from contingent payment plan during their commissions from sales percentages. For this, the contingent plan payment will support their Performance especially if the marketing staff within the organization are qualified in their job and more able for adding a new idea or performance to ingrate the organization improvement. Like: adding new information software or other similar issue or actions. For this, the organization management needs to select the contingent pay plan, to match the employee performance within it plans and targets. Finally in the profit sharing The organization management is required to select the contingent plan payment especially with groups working Because the team or group are sharing the performance integration for the organization. like: finance department.

Example 6.2

The case of Nucor Corporation

This international organization was focusing about it staff performance in steel manufacturing in a good way, by selecting the contingent pay plan. For example, it offered the worker wages from 16 to 21 dollar per hour, plus the bonus which reflect the soul of motivation in worker performance. For this, if the worker was working more, he-she will get more benefits. For this issue, this organization is selecting the contingent pay plan to support it targets and needs. Like: introducing the steel work for the customers during good quantity and quality which mean without any defect or damage to improve its productions to matching the customer's needs. In the same way, if this organization is selecting the traditional pay plan during it worker performance the worker will Focus about the time more than the steel working in quantity and quality. Finally, this organization should reform it worker, by selecting some performance integrations issues. Like: understanding the organization mission, training to polish the worker's skills in steel manufacturing and support the trends of cross-functional team. Like: assistants or supervisors by improving their contingent payment plan operation, wish supports these organization mechanisms in the productions quality.

(Aguinis, H.)

The measurement

During the complex implementation within the organizations in marketing, productions and manufacturing, every organization is trying to it best to manage the HRM during it integration norms, Because the real capital for the organization is it staff and workers. For this, the modern firms are Trying, to laying the motivation and trust within it performance environment to support the organization to match It targets and needs and to provide more opportunities for the organization to support it outcomes. For this, the drawing of staff integration performance in the organization within some important practical tools. Like: strategic, administrative, informational, development during continuously actions, by applying the concept of performance management system within The HRM activities during the organization performance. For this, the HRM are required to focusing in the serious way, some important issues during the journey of staff improvement to guide the improvement advantages within organization improvement currents. Thus, the organization should support it Values and behaviors, during the staff interactions and performance, by improve the staff ability to understand the organization mission and goals, because the clear understanding of the organization targets, will guide the employee performance to match the organization goals and support the organization out source during the duties coordination between top management & staff. In the same way, the HRM should apply the performance management system in providing the clear information about the job duties and rules to staff to support the organization values. In the same way, they should provide the superiors skills or talent in changing the Working activates or performance to avoid any professional performance leakage during some actions. Like: using the appraisal during performance management norms for more integration and continuously. For example but not limit, "The Malaysian Government is Using the new performances appraisal system to improve the teachers performance without touch their personality and values, especially the Malaysian teachers are related form different roots like, India and China wish making the appraisal more complex issues within the performance environment". **(Rahman, S. A).** In the same way, The organization HRM. should using the strategic planning tools within performance management trends during the organization interactions, to match the markets needs, by appointing the qualified staff and monitoring the markets to match the organizations productions with customers needs and improving the organization Ability to expecting the customer needs. Finally the HRM should support the organization Vision, mission during the improve to staff information and performance, For example," The successful story of farma group, in laying branches during India and Africa and matching the Indian, African customers needs in medical materials because of clear vision of farma and it qualified staff". **(Therese F*).** In the a same way, the using of performance management measurement could support the organization in monitoring & protecting to recommending any missing performance actions, to provide the proper solutions to support the organization performance integration in continually operations, For the example, "the Dutch police organization is using the performance management to avoid the crimes and support its coordination with other government sectors like, parliament." **(Hoogenboezem*)**In the same way, the performance management system will provide more improvement for organization, if the HRM for the organization was selecting the performance management system during clear communication media to introduce all information about the PFM and support the staff skills during their interacting with PMS by the training.

Measurement system

For the measurement system in the organization, The organization management should guide it staff performance during the measuring norms, by doing some actions. Like: monitoring the staff performance or making evolution know and recommend the staff performance interactions, to sweep any negatives issues or the performance leakage within the organization". For an example if we assume that, the evaluations or monitoring are showing some conflict between the staff behaviors. Thus, the organization environment is required to guide the employee behavior within organization performance during several actions. Like: open discussions between staff and organization management or make training to introduce the organization targets and needs, to improve the organization performance. In a same way the Author (**Edward J. Lusk**), Was defining the performance management measurement system, by saying that" In the measurement system, the organization should provide the performance measurement system within it activities to analyze it staff performance to recommending any conflict or gap between the employees performance and organization needs by introducing an flexible currents to match the staff performance and it needs during some actions. Like: introducing clear information about the organization mission and vision to improve the staff ability to improve their performance To match the organization mission or making motivation, to support the organization performance and targets".

R&D performance Management Measurement System

The R&D organization is famous international organization during its electronic productions. In the same way, this international organization has several branches within some nations. Like: US& Korea with Several virtual teams. Like:, engineers and scientist to support it innovation within the international markets, but for the hard Competition in electronics manufacturing and productions between the electronics organizations, the R&D management is decide to support the motivations for the engineers, to support more productions in high qualities to match the international markets needs and improve the company completion in global markets. But the bottom of challenges in this case, is to provide the motivation for engineers within the leakage of appraisal records for the behaviors and the qualitative. Like: monitoring the performance. For this, the R&D organization management was introducing a fit performance management system to improve its ability to match it needs to match it performance in high level with the requirement the financial competition. For this, the management of the R&D organization should be introduced in the good ability and Facilities to provide the proper and practical measurement for the organization performance to reform the engineer's performance.

R&D performance Measurements Frame Work

For this important issue, the performance measurement system should be presented with someone who is qualified to interact with the soul of staff performance during their productions and consuming, to recommending any gap during engineer's performance to provide the proper values for this interactions in fair way to introduced more opportunities for more improvement and integrations during this trend to translate the results and actions within R&D performance. For this, The mechanism of performance measurement in R&D organization should run between Some important parties. Like: Scientist and Engineers, to understanding the engineers and staff behaviors and performance to guide it during some practical methods. Like: Compensation or introducing a continual links, between systemic systems with R&D performance system, by evaluating the staff performance to provide the proper improvement plans. In a same way, I'd like to say that, the introducing of new systemic system within R&D performance, will support this organization performance in continually way, especially if this systemic system is matching the performance improvement in R&D organization. By applying the:

1- Using more researchers about the staff and engineers behaviors and interactions in R&D Environments, to draw a clear frame about the performance measurement system during this organization.

2- Using the performance measurement system to provide more comfortable working environment, especially in introducing the results of evaluations for the staff and engineers performance within advantages currents to provide more opportunities for staff and engineers to reform their performance regarding their duties especially if they are Understand the goals and targets for their organization.

3- Improving the researches and analysis scales by using its outside the R&D organization Especially in understanding what the customers are expecting from R&D organization in its Productions quality and facilities to support the R&D performance to match the customer's requirements and needs,

For those sensitive's and important issues which are mentioned above, the performance measurement system within R&D organization should run during important currents. Like: job satisfaction, involvement system and introducing more researchers and data capitals, to guide the staff behaviors within R&D performance.

Current 1

In this current the management of this organization, using more researchers about the staff and engineers behaviors and interactions in R&D Environments, to draw a clear frame about the performance measurement system during this organization. For example, the analyzing of R&D performance measurement about the links values between the staff performance and performance management measurement system performance during their job satisfied are showing that, 0.314 from R&D organization, are satisfied within this performance measurement system for this the R&D management are required to motivate it staff for this trend by showing them the benefits of this performance measurement to reshape their performance.

Current 2

In this current, the performance management measurement system are required to introduced the best involvement during staff and engineers performance system to support the R&D organization to match and support it outcomes

Current 3

In this current, the performance management measurement system is required to introduce more researches and data capitals about the international staff interactions within their different cultures and values, to improve the R&D organization ability to match the juice of this interactions within it mission and targets, especially in supporting it commercial profits within the international markets. For example, In 1999 the management of R&D organization in Korea branch are using the experiences of many management scholars, to reshape their surveys and questioners about the engineers and staff performance system during modern measurement performance system, to support their feedback within 55 international branches with more than 1024 responding, the analysis of this responding are showing some important points. Like: Missing of data between engineers, staff performance within R&D. For this issue, The management of R&D organization is introducing the trainings and coaching to match the engineers and staff performance with it targets and needs. Thus, The management of R&D organization are passing in nice way, to reform the engineers and staff of this organization in productions and productions consuming, by providing the proper applying for performance management measurement interactions during the evaluating of employees and staff performance and taking the juice of 1000 hypothesis from management scholars in Korea branch, to support and improve the organization management ability to guide the evaluation feedback within practical current for more integration and improvement to support the R&D organization performance. Like: reforming the team work performance by motivating them and improve their communications interactions and support the leadership information & communication skills to support the mission of ideal measurement system. Which improve the continually changing of staff performance & behaviors in positive interactions to improve the R&D organization to meet it outcomes within it integration and commercial markets?

(Omega (2002).
(Jan Kratzer)
(Bowen Kim, Heungshik Oh)

Conclusion:

At the End of my humble effort, I'm wishing from my book to pass in the good way in clarifying and explain the integration currents for HRM. During: establishing, practice and adding some talents actions and behaviors within due some plans. Like: reforming operations for the organizations strategies, to an alliance for the successful norms for the organizations performance and targets. Even if the organization is reforming during demotic or global scales to support it targets and profits, because my book is proposing an obvious scope about the history of HRM, in the middle of eighteen century till our modern contemporary shape for the HRM performance and practices, by focusing about, the staff and workers as important renewable capitals for the organization, and how Did, the HRM sector in the organization, is support the sustainability of this necessary capital during performance and behavior, by draw an clear unconventional strategies for every organization needs, regarding achieve more goals and objectives within clear and honest currents of implementations between organizations. Thus, Nowadays every modern organization should have it own mechanism regarding it performance environment, because of the number and mentalities for it different staff and shared targets in goals and benefits, Therefore, I'm offering the Concept of HRM, within domestic and international scope and mentions some challenges in reforming the organization performance, by measuring the proper needs for some new strategies for the organization. Therefore, I'm measure the organization environment ability for the new strategies accepting journey. from empirical studies till some practical actions to reform the organization power in matching the requirements, of complex implementations, between the organizations, regarding the sustainability and profits. In the same way, the mission of HRM is more complex within international norms within international organization, Because the I-HRM, are interacting and deal with hybrid environment, regarding the difference needs from international customers from the international organization productions and services and the requirements or the conditions for the Host nation to support the mechanism of the new investment, Regarding The international organization activities and productions. For this, the I-HRM, are reflecting the smart techniques in analyzing the international cultures, for the international cultures, with strong foundation, in analyzing the mother culture, or the international organization to support the smart trends for the organization in understanding other organizations performance and cultures, to introduce some flexible current of negations, between the global organizations. In the same way, the HRM are support, the Currents of managing accounting during selecting strategies within flexible currents to support all of the managerial and financial activities to match the integration scope for all of domestics and international organization. Especially in support the organization budgets and avoids any financial crises. Like: inflation or capital leakage.

Best Regards
Qassim
qssm.jml@gmail.com

References

Hired hands or human resources? [electronic book] case studies **of HRM programs and practices in early American industry / Bruce E. Kaufman.** Detail Only AvailableBy: Kaufman, Bruce E.. Ithaca: ILR Press, 2010. 01/01/2010 xi, 254, [11] p.: ill. Language: English.

The theory and practice of strategic HRM and participative management: Antecedents in early industrial relations Original Research Article
Human Resource Management Review, Volume 11, Issue 4, Winter 2001, Pages 505-533
Bruce E. Kaufman

http://ac.els-cdn.com.ezproxy.liv.ac.uk/S1053482201000511/1-s2.0-S1053482201000511-main.pdf?_tid=239f7bc0-22e0-11e3-b217-00000aacb361&acdnat=1379783361_28258b68401d980c19bedf776f0c0efb

Atrill, P. & McLaney, E. (2012) Management Accounting for Decision Makers. 7th ed. Harlow, England: Pearson Education Ltd.

Herman Aguinis,. (2013)Performance management Third ed.USA:

John Robarts. (2007). The Modren Firm.Organization Desing, For Performance And Growth.

Pilbeam, S. & Corbridge, M. (2010) *People resourcing: contemporary HRM in practice.* 4th ed. London: Prentice Hall International.

Amanda Rose. Ethics and Human Recourses Management, (2007) By Talya N. Bauer, Ph.D

http://www.right.com/thought-leadership/research/shrm-foundations-effective-practice-guidelines-series-onboarding-new-employees-maximizing-success-sponsored-by-right-management.pdf (20-3-2014)

An effective R&D performance measurement system: survey of Korean R&D researchers, Bowon Kim*

Heungshik Oh (2002)http://ac.els-cdn.com.ezproxy.liv.ac.uk/S030504830 1000494/1-s2.0-S0305048301000494-main.pdf?_tid=291c61c2-2686-11e3-b82c-00000aacb361&acdnat=1380184520_cc52e797becce61fae29950c7f0a7441

European Management Journal, Volume 9, Issue 1, March 1991, Pages 46-59 Kamran Kashani, Robert Howard. http://ac.els-cdn.com.ezproxy.liv.ac.uk/ 026323739190050Z/1-s2.0-026323739190050Z-main.pdf?_tid=5fb6fc76-9f93-11e2-b282-00000aab0f6b&acdnat=1365346789_81190972c9156747c8 ec20cf50acd5af(accesd in may 2013)

Timothy J.Minchin. Labor History, Vol 48.No3, August 2007.P 327-346 http:// www.tandfonline.com.ezproxy.liv.ac.uk/doi/abs/10.1080/00236560701418062#. UkGHLtIbDho

Police reform in The Netherlands: A dance between national steering and local performing. Full Text Available By: Cachet, Lex; Marks, Peter. *German Policy Studies/ Politikfeldanalyse.* 2009, Vol. 5 Issue 2, p91-115. 25p http://ehis.ebscohost.com. ezproxy.liv.ac.uk/eds/pdfviewer/pdfviewer?sid=ff33f4cf-8790-4f64-9ca3-05b5e e841ee4%40sessionmgr10&vid=1&hid=17

1**Conceptual and methodological issues in comparative HRM research: The Cranet project as an example** Original Research Article
Human Resource Management Review, Volume 21, Issue 1, March 2011, Pages 16-26
Holger Steinmetz, Christian Schwens, Marius Wehner, Rüdiger Kabst-

http://ac.els-cdn.com.ezproxy.liv.ac.uk/S1053482206000829/1-s2.0-S1053482206000829-main.pdf?_tid=70749bf2-f3d7-11e2-a2f2-00000aacb35e&acdnat=1374611922_ff29fa844a8aa4240e9ae0539b85b210

http://ac.els-cdn.com.ezproxy.liv.ac.uk/S0963868713000334/1-s2.0-S0963868713000334-main.pdf?_tid=e62afc94-f3da-11e2-bd7c-00000aab0f6c&acdnat=1374613406_52fa2b365e5b4777cad86ee89132f04

Pilbeam, S. & Corbridge, M. (2010) *People resourcing: contemporary HRM in practice.* 4th ed. London: Prentice Hall International

International Review of Financial Analysis, Volume 15, Issue 3, 2006, Pages 256-286
Erkki K. Laitinen.http://ac.els-cdn.com.ezproxy.liv.ac.uk/S1057521905000384/1-s2.0-S1057521905000384-main.pdf?_tid=83af7b2a-9f94-11e2-b282-00000aab0f6b&acdnat=1365347281_5d82ff91deb14e0e6ecf80c96e5a7917(accesd in may 2013)

International Review of Financial Analysis, Volume 17, Issue 5, December 2008, Pages 805-819
Martin Lally, Steve Swidle.*http://ac.els-cdn.com.ezproxy.liv.ac.uk/S1057521907000610/1-s2.0-S1057521907000610-main.pdf?_tid=06397168-a5c1-11e2-a3a9-00000aab0f01&acdnat=1366026102_37eb98dbc8c5688875e92d57d06502b1*

International Review of Financial Analysis, Volume 15, Issue 3, 2006, Pages 256-286
Erkki K. Laitinen. http://ac.els-cdn.com.ezproxy.liv.ac.uk/S1057521905000384/1-s2.0-S1057521905000384-main.pdf?_tid=c5ff410e-a813-11e2-b0fb-00000aab0f6b&acdnat=1366281545_bc2aef4e30dcd96bf64e600430905d19

Journal of Banking & Finance, Volume 35, Issue 1, January 2011, Pages 182-192
Robert Ferstl, Alex Weissensteine.*http://ac.els-cdn.com.ezproxy.liv.ac.uk/S0167923601001312/1-s2.0-S0167923601001312-main.pdf?_tid=ea348522-ab18-11e2-9509-00000aacb35e*

Chapter 1 - Introduction

Introduction to Human Resource Management (Second Edition), 2005, Pages 1-42
http://ac.els-cdn.com.ezproxy.liv.ac.uk/B9780750665346500032/3-s2.0-B9780750665346500032-main.pdf?_tid=1d8a064c-ef9b-11e2-8faa-00000aacb35e&acdnat=1374146207_75af53829138201f772b6e8836d64a06

A framework for diagnosing human resource management practices Original Research Article
European Management Journal, Volume 14, Issue 3, June 1996, Pages 243-254
Jean-Marie Hiltrop
http://ac.els-cdn.com.ezproxy.liv.ac.uk/0263237396000047/1-s2.0-0263237396000047-main.pdf?_tid=be5e5b76-ef9c-11e2-b289-00000aab0f26&acdnat=1374146909_d738cea54361628266e391ba7f2ea757

-Strategic human resource management: Employee involvement, diversity, and international issues Original Research Article
Human Resource Management Review, Volume 8, Issue 3, Autumn 1998, Pages 193-214
Gary C. McMahan, Myrtle P. Bell, Meghna Virick

http://ac.els-cdn.com.ezproxy.liv.ac.uk/S105348229890002X/1-s2.0-S105348229890002X-main.pdf?_tid=ff76edc6-ef9c-11e2-b289-00000aab0f26&acdnat=1374147015_094918dcaf3deb82babbfa58dd08dc4c

The impact of cultural values on the acceptance and effectiveness of human resource management policies and practices Original Research Article
*Human Resource Management Review, Volume 17, Issue 2, June 2007, Pages 152-165*Dianna L. Stone, Eugene F. Stone-Romero, Kimberly M. Lukaszewsk

http://ac.els-cdn.com.ezproxy.liv.ac.uk/S105348220700023X/1-s2.0-S105348220700023X-main.pdf?_tid=9a5828fa-ef9d-11e2-b289-00000aab0f26&acdnat=1374147275_59a52458bbb11f8f55d39c2bb7504e7d

CHAPTER 10 - Organising and Human Resource Management

Managing Football, 2010, Pages 169-184
Dr Linda Trenberth

http://ac.els-cdn.com.ezproxy.liv.ac.uk/B9781856175449000102/3-s2.0-B9781856175449000102-main.pdf?_tid=a11b9270-efa3-11e2-aff7-00000aacb360&acdnat=1374149863_69f724911020a2687a738ef6ae49921e

Human resources management: some new directions Original Research Article
Journal of Management, Volume 25, Issue 3, 1999, Pages 385-415
Gerald R Ferris, Wayne A Hochwarter, M.Ronald Buckley, Gloria Harrell-Cook, Dwight D Frink

http://ac.els-cdn.com.ezproxy.liv.ac.uk/S0149206399000070/1-s2.0-S0149206399000070-main.pdf?_tid=ff531a02-efa3-11e2-a5da-00000aab0f27&acdnat=1374150021_f93f5b17801fff8d7f409f6e32b9989f

Conceptual and methodological issues in comparative HRM research: The Cranet project as an example Original Research Article
Human Resource Management Review, Volume 21, Issue 1, March 2011, Pages 16-26
Holger Steinmetz, Christian Schwens, Marius Wehner, Rüdiger Kabs

http://ac.els-cdn.com.ezproxy.liv.ac.uk/S1053482210000446/1-s2.0-S1053482210000446-main.pdf?_tid=f3c2df7e-ed32-11e2-82af-00000aacb362&acdnat=1373881567_98a769a2d89934b862cdf3b97d1c01ae

-European Management Journal, Volume 26, Issue 3, June 2008, Pages 153-165
Tanya V. Bondarouk, Huub J.M. Ruël

http://ac.els-cdn.com.ezproxy.liv.ac.uk/S0263237308000194/1-s2.0-S0263237308000194-main.pdf?_tid=b1bb1a3c-ed33-11e2-82af-00000aacb362&acdnat=1373881885_794b2f21a934d12e80e811a224385b6f

European Management Journal, Volume 24, Issue 4, August 2006, Pages 288-298
Loïc Cadin, Francis Guérin, Robert DeFillipp

http://ac.els-cdn.com.ezproxy.liv.ac.uk/S0263237306000314/1-s2.0-S0263237306000314-main.pdf?_tid=c01874ac-ed34-11e2-aa59-00000aab0f26&acdnat=1373882339_94b8991232a41d0f858a4f548476d7c5

-Human Resource Management, Psychology of
International Encyclopedia of the Social & Behavioral Sciences, 2001, Pages 7003-7007
W.F. Cascio

http://ac.els-cdn.com.ezproxy.liv.ac.uk/B0080430767014078/3-s2.0-B0080430767014078-main.pdf?_tid=6547d248-ed48-11e2-b90b-00000aacb35e&acdnat=1373890776_fd2e16604f5d2cf27521e22ac3ca3f2a

Chapter 1 - Challenges Facing the Employment Relationship: Introduction
The Employment Relationship, 2003, Pages 1-27

http://ac.els-cdn.com.ezproxy.liv.ac.uk/B9780750649414500053/3-s2.0-B9780750649414500053-main.pdf?_tid=fba11308-ed48-11e2-b90b-00000aacb35e&acdnat=1373891029_aef9dd4dfebfe10703dc409fe133ec45

International Business Review, Volume 17, Issue 2, April 2008, Pages 146-158
Ingmar Björkman, Adam Smale, Jennie Sumelius, Vesa Suutari, Yuan Lu

http://ac.els-cdn.com.ezproxy.liv.ac.uk/S0969593108000103/1-s2.0-S0969593108000103-main.pdf?_tid=0dcb90f6-ed4b-11e2-a99a-00000aacb35e&acdnat=1373891918_6d447c3a2abbf7c62863f53b3db57052

-Examining the differential use of global integration mechanisms across HRM practices: Evidence from China Original Research Article
Journal of World Business, Volume 48, Issue 2, April 2013, Pages 232-240
Adam Smale, Ingmar Björkman, Jennie Sumelius

http://ac.els-cdn.com.ezproxy.liv.ac.uk/S1090951612000600/1-s2.0-S1090951612000600-main.pdf?_tid=afd3153a-eedc-11e2-8758-00000aacb361&acdnat=1374064418_4847f321760e733006677ce51987065a

-Contextualizing HRM in comparative research: The role of the Cranet network Original Research Article. *Human Resource Management Review, Volume 21, Issue 1, March 2011, Pages 37-49*
Koen Dewettinck, Jonathan Remue

http://ac.els-cdn.com.ezproxy.liv.ac.uk/S105348221000046X/1-s2.0-S105348221000046X-main.pdf?_tid=090841a2-eedd-11e2-8758-00000aacb361&acdnat=1374064568_f03032e4cae30aa3f7e74e93c62778ea

-A process perspective on transnational HRM systems — A dynamic capability-based analysis Original Research Article
Human Resource Management Review, Volume 21, Issue 3, September 2011, Pages 162-173 Marion Festing, Judith Eidems

http://ac.els-cdn.com.ezproxy.liv.ac.uk/S1053482211000039/1-s2.0-S1053482211000039-main.pdf?_tid=96737d9a-eedd-11e2-8758-00000aacb361&acdnat=1374064805_3469ebe0409c4859e1ca7f8be8d870d3

-Changes in institutional context and MNC operations in China: Subsidiary HRM practices in 1996 versus 2006 Original Research Article
International Business Review, Volume 17, Issue 2, April 2008, Pages 146-158
Ingmar Björkman, Adam Smale, Jennie Sumelius, Vesa Suutari, Yuan Lu

http://ac.els-cdn.com.ezproxy.liv.ac.uk/S0969593108000103/1-s2.0-S0969593108000103-main.pdf?_tid=ce33e18e-eedd-11e2-8758-00000aacb361&acdnat=1374064899_cc9b0eb8a1387c5ad02186efd11e6c91

How job-level HRM effectiveness influences employee intent to turnover and workarounds in hospitals Original Research Article
Journal of Business Research, Volume 65, Issue 4, April 2012, Pages 547-554

Anthony R. Wheeler, Jonathon R.B. Halbesleben, Kenneth J. Harris

http://ac.els-cdn.com.ezproxy.liv.ac.uk/S0148296311000531/1-s2.0-S0148296311000531-main.pdf?_tid=4cf80612-eede-11e2-8758-00000aacb361&acdnat=1374065111_7670c9170fb1015de34fa6ca82ec30d0

- Strategic HRM in building micro-foundations of organizational knowledge-based performance Original Research Article
Human Resource Management Review, In Press, Corrected Proof, Available online 16 November 2012 Dana B. Minbaeva

http://ac.els-cdn.com.ezproxy.liv.ac.uk/S1053482212000836/1-s2.0-S1053482212000836-main.pdf?_tid=e1c2dca4-eede-11e2-8758-00000aacb361&acdnat=1374065362_c5ed4381383b17bf4c6625963e354603

- The theory and practice of strategic HRM and participative management: Antecedents in early industrial relations Original Research Article
Human Resource Management Review, Volume 11, Issue 4, Winter 2001, Pages 505-533
Bruce E. Kaufman

http://ac.els-cdn.com.ezproxy.liv.ac.uk/S1053482201000511/1-s2.0-S1053482201000511-main.pdf?_tid=2b09dba6-eedf-11e2-8354-00000aacb35d&acdnat=1374065484_440e52fee563ad0a0258855b52e8b08c

Strategic human resource management, market orientation, and organizational performance Original Research Article
Journal of Business Research, Volume 51, Issue 2, February 2001, Pages 157-166
Lloyd C. Harris, Emmanuel Ogbonna

http://ac.els-cdn.com.ezproxy.liv.ac.uk/S0148296399000570/1-s2.0-S0148296399000570-main.pdf?_tid=5a016eb0-eedf-11e2-8354-00000aacb35d&acdnat=1374065563_a9b2cad30ab9dd9e21a9a111b336504a

-High Performance Work Systems and Intermediate Indicators of Firm Performance Within the US Small Business Sector Original Research Article
Journal of Management, Volume 28, Issue 6, December 2002, Pages 765-785
Sean A. Way

http://ac.els-cdn.com.ezproxy.liv.ac.uk/S0149206302001915/1-s2.0-S0149206302001915-main.pdf?_tid=8b4e7c92-eedf-11e2-8354-00000aacb35d&acdnat=1374065645_d021ddcd48f92c61ad594494a52c56b5

-Measuring HRM effectiveness: Considering multiple stakeholders in a global context Original Research Article
Human Resource Management Review, Volume 16, Issue 2, June 2006, Pages 209-218
Saba Colakoglu, David P. Lepak, Ying Hong

http://ac.els-cdn.com.ezproxy.liv.ac.uk/S1053482206000180/1-s2.0-S1053482206000180-main.pdf?_tid=eecb647e-eedf-11e2-8354-00000aacb35d&acdnat=1374065812_724a8d5bf11ef3b875de8329c6f447fc

-Validating the human resource system structure: A levels-based strategic HRM approach Original Research Article
Human Resource Management Review, Volume 17, Issue 1, March 2007, Pages 77-92
Jeffrey B. Arthur, Trish Boyles

http://ac.els-cdn.com.ezproxy.liv.ac.uk/S1053482207000046/1-s2.0-S1053482207000046-main.pdf?_tid=240ccdd0-eee0-11e2-8354-00000aacb35d&acdnat=1374065902_989e19e00264138cceadab4221aa52e3

- The value of human resource management for organizational performance Original Research Article
Business Horizons, Volume 50, Issue 6, November–December 2007, Pages 503-511
Yongmei Liu, James G. Combs, David J. Ketchen Jr., R. Duane Ireland

http://ac.els-cdn.com.ezproxy.liv.ac.uk/S0007681307000833/1-s2.0-S0007681307000833-main.pdf?_tid=9be8e05a-eee0-11e2-8354-00000aacb35d&acdnat=1374066103_df3724e34c0f62ab2d7a38cfe0941557

-HRM practices affecting extrinsic and intrinsic motivation of knowledge receivers and their effect on intra-MNC knowledge transfer Original Research Article
International Business Review, Volume 17, Issue 6, December 2008, Pages 703-713
Dana B. Minbaeva

http://ac.els-cdn.com.ezproxy.liv.ac.uk/S0969593108000899/1-s2.0-S0969593108000899-main.pdf?_tid=339f0db6-eee1-11e2-8354-00000aacb35d&acdnat=1374066360_57d2a9eb34f4b7769f2c014e7f585197

The impact of downsizing on trust and employee practices in high tech firms: A longitudinal analysis Original Research Article
The Journal of High Technology Management Research, Volume 16, Issue 2, December 2005, Pages 193-207
Shay S. Tzafrir, Merav Eitam-Meilik

http://ac.els-cdn.com.ezproxy.liv.ac.uk/S1047831005000209/1-s2.0-S1047831005000209-main.pdf?_tid=8c5c22ae-eee1-11e2-8354-00000aacb35d&acdnat=1374066508_613f019243bef1670d56f7fc6e309e53

-Strategic human resource management: The evolution of the field Original
Human Resource Management Review, Volume 19, Issue 2, June 2009, Pages 64-85
Mark L. Lengnick-Hall, Cynthia A. Len

http://ac.els-cdn.com.ezproxy.liv.ac.uk/S1053482209000035/1-s2.0-S1053482209000035-main.pdf?_tid=bfc020d2-eee1-11e2-8354-00000aacb35d&acdnat=1374066592_70a39ee725ecb62d466fcd3a9702c783

Wu, Congsheng; Chinese Economy, September-October 2011, v. 44, iss. 5, pp. 104-19
Vincent Bouvatier. Applied Economics, 2010, 42, 1533-1548.
Chunxia Jiang and Shujie YAO.China Economic Review, 20,(2009),717 – 731.

Training Knowledge Workers ©APO 2004, ISBN: 92-833-7029-5 (02-RP-GE-SUV-02) Report of the APO Survey on In-Company Training Strategies for Knowledge Workersructure.html#ixzz1LrlISMOj

http://www.huffingtonpost.com/2011/09/12/bank-of-america-to-cut-30_n_958432.html

What is the meaning of 'talent' in the world of work? Original Research Article
Human Resource Management Review, In Press, Corrected Proof, Available online 29 May 2013 Eva Gallardo-Gallardo, Nicky Dries, Tomás F. González-Cruz

http://ac.els-cdn.com.ezproxy.liv.ac.uk/S1053482213000302/1-s2.0-S1053482213000302-main.pdf?_tid=3debe2a2-eee2-11e2-9065-00000aacb35d&acdnat=1374066804_39cacdcfa18af97276eb018098a3eeba

Talent — Innate or acquired? Theoretical considerations and their implications for talent management Original Research Article
*Human Resource Management Review, In Press, Corrected Proof, Available online 28 May 2013*M. Christina Meyers, Marianne van Woerkom, Nicky Dries

-Developing tomorrow's leaders—Evidence of global talent management in multinational enterprises Original Research Article
Journal of World Business, Volume 45, Issue 2, April 2010, Pages 150-160
Anthony McDonnell, Ryan Lamare, Patrick Gunnigle, Jonathan Lavelle

http://ac.els-cdn.com.ezproxy.liv.ac.uk/S1090951609000765/1-s2.0-S1090951609000765-main.pdf?_tid=de2d6f06-eee2-11e2-96cf-00000aacb362&acdnat=1374067073_7b0947d46b8b752b93b1104445f41290

-Personel Selection based on Talent Management Original Research Article
Procedia - Social and Behavioral Sciences, Volume 73, 27 February 2013, Pages 68-72
Erdem Aksakal, Metin Dağdeviren, Ergün Eraslan, İhsan Yüksel

http://ac.els-cdn.com.ezproxy.liv.ac.uk/S1877042813003145/1-s2.0-S1877042813003145-main.pdf?_tid=337535a2-eee3-11e2-81bd-00000aab0f6c&acdnat=1374067216_0963719e754946ce7f12b9efcf701b47

-Strategic talent management: A review and research agenda Original Research
Human Resource Management Review, Volume 19, Issue 4, December 2009, Pages 304-313 David G. Collings, Kamel Mellahi

http://ac.els-cdn.com.ezproxy.liv.ac.uk/S1053482209000461/1-s2.0-S1053482209000461-main.pdf?_tid=888ae1ea-eee3-11e2-81bd-00000aab0f6c&acdnat=1374067361_af08800966315ae4b6a11065996bc5a5

-The Effects of Using Talent Management With Performance Evaluation System Over Employee Commitment Original Research Article
Procedia - Social and Behavioral Sciences, Volume 58, 12 October 2012, Pages 340-349
Yalçın Vural, Pelin Vardarlier, Abdullah Aykir

http://ac.els-cdn.com.ezproxy.liv.ac.uk/S1877042812044710/1-s2.0-S1877042812044710-main.pdf?_tid=e7b706e4-eee3-11e2-81bd-00000aab0f6c&acdnat=1374067518_1e630f46382617cb1a06f16b3d51fd8e

Designing a model for managing talents of students in elementary school: A qualitative study based on grounded theory Original Research Article
Procedia - Social and Behavioral Sciences, Volume 29, 2011, Pages 1052-1060
Fahimeh Veladat, Abdolrahim Navehebrahim

http://ac.els-cdn.com.ezproxy.liv.ac.uk/S1877042811027996/1-s2.0-S1877042811027996-main.pdf?_tid=2b87f8ce-eee4-11e2-8eb1-00000aacb362&acdnat=1374067632_38934f80449bb40c407b3f6438e7c2ae

http://ac.els-cdn.com.ezproxy.liv.ac.uk/S1053482204000178/1-s2.0-S1053482204000178-main.pdf?_tid=c3e41686-efaa-11e2-9e64-00000aab0f02&acdnat=1374152928_d1e5560cc2820e39be88bbbc9fca7e81

Talent management of western MNCs in China: Balancing global integration and local responsiveness Original Research Article
Journal of World Business, Volume 45, Issue 2, April 2010, Pages 169-178
Evi Hartmann, Edda Feisel, Holger Schober

http://ac.els-cdn.com.ezproxy.liv.ac.uk/S1090951609000741/1-s2.0-S1090951609000741-main.pdf?_tid=97df4352-efab-11e2-9e64-00000aab0f02&acdnat=1374153284_de3c9d78f143379285e4d22d3e52d65d

- Strategic talent management: A review and research agenda Original Research Arti
Human Resource Management Review, Volume 19, Issue 4, December 2009, Pages 304-313 David G. Collings, Kamel Mellahi

http://ac.els-cdn.com.ezproxy.liv.ac.uk/S1053482209000461/1-s2.0-S1053482209000461-main.pdf?_tid=68ffb26e-efac-11e2-9e64-00000aab0f02&acdnat=1374153635_f5b7e7400d1c247476bfb397a29023cf

Validating the human resource system structure: A levels-based strategic HRM approach Original Research Article
Human Resource Management Review, Volume 17, Issue 1, March 2007, Pages 77-92
Jeffrey B. Arthur, Trish Boyles

http://ac.els-cdn.com.ezproxy.liv.ac.uk/S1053482207000046/1-s2.0-S1053482207000046-main.pdf?_tid=43c75612-efae-11e2-9285-00000aab0f01&acdnat=1374154431_3fd01ad6d9d9d644815e0c17ba04cbec

Chapter 4 - Measuring the Impact of Strategic HRM

Aligning Human Resources and Business Strategy (Second Edition), 2009, Pages 89-123
Linda Holbeche

http://ac.els-cdn.com.ezproxy.liv.ac.uk/B9780750680172000048/3-s2.0-B9780750680172000048-main.pdf?_tid=546a9bac-f074-11e2-a20b-00000aab0f6b&acdnat=1374239499_98cf632603a9a95f89895d76886a0f60

The role of perceived organizational justice in shaping the outcomes of talent management: A research agenda Original Research Article
Human Resource Management Review, In Press, Corrected Proof, Available online 27 May 2013
Jolyn Gelens, Nicky Dries, Joeri Hofmans, Roland Pepermans

http://ac.els-cdn.com.ezproxy.liv.ac.uk/S1053482213000338/1-s2.0-S1053482213000338-main.pdf?_tid=a4ddd9fa-f074-11e2-a20b-00000aab0f6b&acdnat=1374239634_77dc66374b624a997e43748ceaa7cdfc

Atrill, P. & McLaney, E. (2012) Management Accounting for Decision Makers. 7th ed. Harlow, England: Pearson Education Ltd
Neale G. O'Connora,* Chee W. Chowb, Handbooks of Management Accounting Research, Volume 2, 2006, Pages 923-967.

JOHN EDMUNDS, European Management Journal, Volume 16, Issue 2, April 1998.
Scapens, R.W. (2006) 'Understanding management accounting practices: a personal journey', The British Accounting Review, 38 (1), pp. 1–30, Elsevier

Hall, M. (2010) 'Accounting information and managerial work' Accounting, Organizations and Society, 35 (3), pp. 301-315
Journal of Banking & Finance, Volume 27, Issue 7, July 2003, Pages 1219-1243
Ronald E Shrieves, Drew Dah

Atrill, P. & McLaney, E. (2012) Management Accounting for Decision Makers. 7th ed. Harlow, England: Pearson Education Ltd

Lucas, M. & Rafferty, J. (2008) 'Cost analysis for pricing: exploring the gap between theory and practice', The British Accounting Review, 40 (2), pp. 148–160

Journal of Cleaner Production, Volume 11, Issue 6, September 2003, Pages 667-676
Christine Jasch.

Food Policy, Volume 36, Issue 2, April 2011, Pages 204-213
Joakim Gullstrand

Journal of Air Transport Management, Volume 11, Issue 5, September 2005, Pages 303-312
Peter Morrell

Pong, C. & Mitchell, F. (2006) 'Full costing versus variable costing: does the choice still matter? An empirical exploration of UK manufacturing companies 1988–2002', The British Accounting Review, 38 (2), pp. 131–148, Elsevier SD Freedom Collection [Online]. DOI: 10.1016/j.bar.2005.09.003 (Accessed 30 June 2009).

*GIUSEPPE DI GRAZIANO *.International Journal of Theoretical and Applied Finance*
Vol. 15, No. 1 (2012).

Structural Change and Economic Dynamics, Volume 19, Issue 1, March 2008, Pages 17-37
Christian Bellak, Markus Albrecht, Aleksandra Riedl

Evaluation and Program Planning, Volume 35, Issue 3, August 2012, Pages 303-320
Hung-Yi Wu

European Journal of Operational Research, Volume 196, Issue 3, 1 August 2009, Pages 1177-1189

*Teresa García-Valderrama, Eva Mulero-Mendigorri, Daniel Revuelta-*Bordo

Klammer, T, & Wilner, N 1991, 'Capital budgeting practices--a survey of corporate use', Journal Of Management Accounting Research, 3, pp. 113-130, Business Source Premier, EBSCOhost,

Royal FrieslandCampina, 2012. [Online]

Available at: http://www.frieslandcampina.com/english/news-and-press/news/press-releases/2012-05-22-frieslandcampina-press-release.aspx.

Information & Management, Volume 39, Issue 4, January 2002, Pages 271-281

James S.K Ang, Chee-Chuong Sum, Lei-Noy Yeo. http://ac.els-cdn.com.ezproxy.liv.ac.uk/S0378720601000969/1-s2.0-S0378720601000969-main.pdf?tid=b7e948ee-ae44-11e2-ab44-00000aab0f6c&acdnat=1366962274_875204 a7b06d87cb4a5fda8d234df3cc

Atrill, P. & McLaney, E. (2012) Management Accounting for Decision Makers. 7th ed. Harlow, England: Pearson Education Ltd.
European Management Journal, Volume 9, Issue 1, March 1991, Pages 46-59

Kamran Kashani, Robert Howard. http://ac.els-cdn.com.ezproxy.liv.ac.uk/026323739190050Z/1-s2.0-026323739190050Z-main.pdf?tid=5fb6fc76-9f93-11e2-b282-00000aab0f6b&acdnat=1365346789_811909 72c9156747c8ec20cf50acd5af(accesd in may 2013)
International Review of Financial Analysis, Volume 15, Issue 3, 2006, Pages 256-286

Erkki K. Laitinen.http://ac.els-cdn.com.ezproxy.liv.ac.uk/S1057521905000384/1-s2.0-S1057521905000384-main.pdf?_tid=83af7b2a-9f94-11e2-b282-00000aa

b0f6b&acdnat=1365347281_5d82ff91deb14e0e6ecf80c96e5a7917(accesd in may 2013)
International Review of Financial Analysis, Volume 17, Issue 5, December 2008, Pages 805-819

Martin Lally, Steve Swidle.*http://ac.els-cdn.com.ezproxy.liv.ac.uk/ S1057521907000610/1-s2.0-S1057521907000610-main.pdf?_tid=06397168- a5c1-11e2-a3a9-00000aab0f01&acdnat=1366026102_37eb98dbc8c5688875 e92d57d06502b1*
International Review of Financial Analysis, Volume 15, Issue 3, 2006, Pages 256-286

Erkki K. Laitinen. *http://ac.els-cdn.com.ezproxy.liv.ac.uk/S1057521905000384/1- s2.0-S1057521905000384-main.pdf?_tid=c5ff410e-a813-11e2-b0fb- 00000aab0f6b&acdnat=1366281545_bc2aef4e30dcd96bf64e600430905d19*
Journal of Banking & Finance, Volume 35, Issue 1, January 2011, Pages 182-192

Robert Ferstl, Alex Weissensteine.*http://ac.els-cdn.com.ezproxy.liv.ac.uk/S016 7923601001312/1-s2.0-S0167923601001312-main.pdf?_ tid=ea348522-ab18-11e2-9509-00000aacb35e&acdnat=1366613609_ eb2605e42cd4ce93897f4c03cd41b0e7*

Richard Mead & Tim G.Andrews. International Management, Fourth Edition

Michael Naor.Journal of operations management 28 (2010)194-205

Frank B. International Journal of Cross Cultural Management. 2009 Vol 9(2): 145–168.

Barry wilkiionson. Organization Studies, May 1996; vol. 17, 3: pp. 421-447.2

Bird, A. & Fang, T. (2009) 'Editorial: cross cultural management in the age of globalization', International Journal of Cross Cultural Management, 9 (2), pp. 139–142.

Chevrier, S. (2009) 'Is national culture still relevant to management in a global context? The case of Switzerland', International Journal of Cross Cultural Management, 9 (2), pp.169–181

Richard Mead & Tim G.Andrews. International Management, Fourth Edition

HyoSun Jung. International Journal of hospitality management 29 (2010) 538-546

Giorgos Papaginnakis. Journal of Environmental management 10092012041-51

Lane Kelly. Journal of International management 12 (2006) 67-84

Lynn E. Metcalf. Journal of world business 41 (2006) 382-394

Chao C. Chen Journal of management 2002 28 (4) 567-583

Chan –Hoong leong International journal on intercultural relations 30 2006 799 - 810

Stacey R. Fitzsimmons, Christof Miska, Gü̈nter K. Stahl. Organizational Dynamics (2011) 40, 199—206

Brett, Jeanne, Behfar, Kristin, Kern, Mary C. Harvard Business Review; Nov2006, Vol. 84 Issue 11, p84-91, 8p, 2 Illustrations.

Lee, M.R. (2009) 'E-ethical leadership for virtual project teams', International Journal of Project Management, 27 (5), pp.456-463. DOI: 10.1016/j.ijproman.2008.05.012

Symons, J. & Stenzel, C. (2007) 'Virtually borderless: an examination of culture in virtual teaming', Journal of General Management, 32 (3), pp.1-17,

Brett, J., Behfar, K. & Kern, M. (2006) 'Managing multicultural teams', Harvard Business Review, 84 (11), pp.84-91

Yi Chen, Dean Tjosvold. Journal of international management 11(2005) 417-439

Matthias Neuenkirch. European Journal of Political Economy 28 (2012) 1–13

Thomas Oosthuizen. (2004) 'In marketing across cultures: are you enlightening the, 20 (2), 61–72, (Accessed: 23 December 2009).

Jacques Melitz. European Economic Review 52 (2008) 667–699

Taylor, S. (2007) 'Creating social capital in MNCs: the international human resource management challenge', Human Resource Management Journal, 17 (4), pp. 336–354, Wiley InterScience [Online]. DOI:10.1111/j.1748-8583.2007.00049.x (Accessed: 23 December 2009).

http://dx.doi.org.ezproxy.liv.ac.uk/10.1111/j.1748-8583.2007.00049.x

Asif Dowla. The Journal of Socio-Economics 35 (2006) 102–122

Ralston, D.A. (2007) 'The Crossvergence perspective: reflections and projections', Journal of International Business Studies, 39 (1), pp. 27–40, Palgrave Macmillan [Online]. DOI:10.1057/palgrave.jibs.8400333 (Accessed: 23 December 2009).

http://dx.doi.org.ezproxy.liv.ac.uk/10.1057/palgrave.jibs.8400333

Richard Mead & Tim G.Andrews. International Management, Fourth Edition

International Business Review, Volume 19, Issue 4, August 2010, Pages 419-431

Shaista E. Khilji, Nurit Zeidman, Amos Drory, Aqeel Tirmizi

Ghauri, P. & Fang, T. (1999) The Chinese business negotiation process: a socio-cultural analysis [online]. Available from:

http://som.eldoc.ub.rug.nl/FILES/reports/1995-1999/themeB/1999/99B15/99b15.pdf

Human Resource Management Review, Volume 21, Issue 2, June 2011, Pages 123-136
Jamie A. Grumman, Alan M. Saks.

Industrial Marketing Management, Volume 38, Issue 2, February 2009, Pages 152-158
Yu-Shan Chen, Ming-Ji James Lin, Ching-Hsun Chang

Aguinis, H. (2013) Performance management. 3rd ed. Upper Saddle River, NJ: Pearson/Prentice Hall.

Journal of Banking & Finance, Volume 33, Issue 1, January 2009, Pages 39-52
Xiaoping (Maggie) Fu, Shelagh Heffernan

Nankervis, R. A., & Compton, R. L. (2006) 'Performance management: theory in practice?', Asia Pacific Journal of Human Resources, 44 (1), pp. 83–101.

Nankervis, R. A., & Compton, R. L. (2006) 'Performance management: theory in practice?', Asia Pacific Journal of Human Resources, 44 (1), pp. 83–101.

http://sfx7.exlibrisgroup.com.ezproxy.liv.ac.uk/lpu?title=Asia+Pacific+Journal+of+Human+Resources&volume=44&issue=1&spage=83&date=2006&issn=&eissn

Aguinis, H. (2013) Performance management. 3rd

European Journal of Operational Research, Volume 207, Issue 2, 1 December 2010, Pages 971-979, Cheng-Ru Wu, Chin-Tsai Lin, Pei-Hsuan Tsai

The Journal of Strategic Information Systems, In Press, Corrected Proof, Available online 5 June 2012 John M. Ward

Performance management and employee engagement Original Research Article

Human Resource Management Review, Volume 21, Issue 2, June 2011, Pages 123-136
Jamie A. Grumman, Alan M. Saks.

Rahman, S. A. (2006) 'Attitudes of Malaysian teachers toward a performance-appraisal system', Journal of Applied Social Psychology, 36 (12), pp. 3031–3042.

http://sfx7.exlibrisgroup.com.ezproxy.liv.ac.uk/lpu?title=Journal+of+Applied+Social+Psychology&volume=36&issue=12&spage=3031&date=2006

Journal of Engineering and Technology Management, Volume 15, Issue 4, September 1998, Pages 279-308 Holger Ernst

Aguinis, H. (2013) Performance management. 3rd ed. Upper Saddle River, NJ: Pearson/Prentice Hall.

Tapinos, E., Dyson, R. G., & Meadows, M. (2005) 'The impact of performance measurement in strategic planning', International Journal of Productivity and Performance Management, 54 (5-6), pp. 370–384.

http://sfx7.exlibrisgroup.com.ezproxy.liv.ac.uk/lpu?title=International+Journal+of+Productivity+and+Performance+Management&volume=54&issue

Jan Kratzer*, Roger Th.A.J. Leenders, Jo M.L. Van Engelen. Technovation 26 (2006) 42–

Organizational Dynamics, Volume 18, Issue 2, Autumn 1989, Pages 16-32
Roger D. Evered, James C. Selman

Rahman, S. A. (2006) 'Attitudes of Malaysian teachers toward a performance-appraisal system', Journal of Applied Social Psychology, 36 (12), pp. 3031–3042.

http://sfx7.exlibrisgroup.com.ezproxy.liv.ac.uk/lpu?title=Journal+of+Applied+Social+Psychology&volume=36&issue=12&spage=3031&date=2006

Aguinis, H. (2013) Performance management. 3rd ed. Upper Saddle River, NJ: Pearson/Prentice Hall.

*Therese F.Yaeger and peter F.Sorensen. OD.practitioner. Vol.43 No.1 (2011). Jan Kratzer *, Technovation.(2006) 42-49*

Hoogenboezem, J. A., & Hoogenboezem, D. (2005) 'Coping with targets: performance measurement in The Netherlands police', International Journal of Productivity and Performance Management, 54 (7), pp. 568–578.

Omega, Volume 30, Issue 1, February 2002, Pages 19-31
Bowon Kim, Heungshik Oh

Fuzzy Sets and systems, Volume 5, Issue 2, March 1981, Pages 149-157
Edward J. Lusk

Singh, A., & Muncherji, N. (2007) 'Team effectiveness and its measurement: a framework', Global Business Review, 8 (1), pp. 119–133. http://sfx7.exlibrisgroup.com.ezproxy.liv.ac.uk/lpu?title=Global+Business+Review&volume=8&issue=1&spage=119&date=2007&issn=&eissn.

www.ingramcontent.com/pod-product-compliance
Lightning Source LLC
Chambersburg PA
CBHW030750180526
45163CB00003B/969